C000120974

OVER THE RAINBOW BRIDGE

First Impression – 2004

ISBN 0-9548019-0-3

© Wendy M. Tugby

Published by Wendy M. Tugby

British Library Cataloguing-in-Publication Data
A catalogue record for this book is available from the British Library.

All rights reserved. No part of this book may be reproduced, stored in a retrieval system, or transmitted in any form or by any means, electronic, electrostatic, magnetic tape, mechanical, photocopying, recording or otherwise, without permission in writing from the publisher Wendy M. Tugby, Penlleinau, Blaencaron, Tregaron SY25 6HL.

Printed in Wales at
Gomer Press, Llandysul, Ceredigion SA44 4JL

Over the Rainbow Bridge

Wendy M. Tugby

To Sweep,
without whose presence, before and after,
this book would not have been written.

Acknowledgements

Firstly, my thanks to Steve, my partner, for allowing me to recount our experiences and share them with others. Sweep was his dog and he is the one to whom Sweep has appeared. I have been merely a privileged observer on each occasion.

Secondly, my thanks to Jane Lilley, writer of the 'Living With Dogs' column for *Dog World* magazine, to whom I turned for assistance in soliciting contributions for the book. Her help, enthusiasm and encouragement have been invaluable.

Next, a huge 'thank you', to all who contributed ADC experiences for this book. I know that for many of you it wasn't easy and for some it was breaking years of silence. To tell a complete stranger such personal details, knowing that, ultimately, they are going to be shared with goodness knows how many others, is a true leap of faith. Thank you for trusting me. I hope I've done your accounts justice.

Thanks to Sterling Publishing Co. Inc., for granting permission for me to use the extract from *Spirit Medicine* by Wolf Moondance and to Jack Angelo for his permission to use the extract from *Your Healing Power*, published by Piatkus.

Extract from *Proud Spirit* by Rosemary Altea published by Rider. Used by permission of The Random House Group Limited. My thanks to them also.

Contents

The Rainbow Bridge

'Just this side of Heaven is a place called the Rainbow Bridge. When a hound dies that has been especially close to someone here, that dog goes to Rainbow Bridge. There are meadows and hills for all our special friends so they run and play together. There is plenty of food and water and sunshine and our friends are warm and comfortable. All the hounds that are old or ill are restored to health and vigour. Those who were hurt or maimed are made whole and strong again, just as we remember them in our dreams of days and times gone by.

The hounds are happy and content except for one small thing – they each miss someone special to them who had to be left behind. They all run and play together but the day comes when one suddenly stops and looks into the distance. The bright eyes are intent, the eager body quivers. Suddenly he begins to run from the group, flying over the green grass, his legs carrying him faster and faster. YOU have been spotted and when you and your special friend finally meet, you cling together in joyous reunion, never to be parted again. The happy kisses rain upon your face, your hands again caress the beloved head and you look once more into the trusting eyes of your hound so long gone from your life but never absent from your heart. Then you cross the Rainbow Bridge together.'

Anon.

*   *   *

The Rainbow Bridge poem will be familiar to many of you. To Native American (Shaman) Indians, the Rainbow Bridge is known as the way into the spirit world.

*   *   *

'Someday, when the road darkens and you drop your physical robe and die a physical death, you will cross over the Rainbow Bridge and there the spirit horse will wait for you and carry you home.'

From *Spirit Medicine*, by Wolf Moondance

Introduction

At the end of February 2003, my partner Steve and I lost a favourite hound. His name was Sweep. We were grief-stricken and traumatised by his loss, which was both sudden and totally unexpected and made worse by the fact that he was only 22 months old.

There will be many of you that have lost, not just dogs but pet animals of all kinds, who will understand how we felt at that time. There is nothing that can be said, nothing that can be done, to ease the pain and emptiness when they leave. For so many it is the loss of a dearly loved friend, and so it was for us.

But; sometimes there is something that helps. Sometimes we are fortunate enough to have our departed friends make contact with us from the other side, which is exactly what happened in our case and the reason this book came into being. As hard as it was at first, to believe what was happening, happen it did and our experiences have been validated time and time again by the many who have contributed to this book and to whom we extend our everlasting gratitude.

* * *

Thankfully, when I first realized that something 'unusual' was going on, I started to keep a record of events in a diary. So much was happening and so quickly, that I knew I couldn't trust it all to memory.

One thing in particular that was becoming increasingly apparent was the comfort and emotional and spiritual healing we were getting from it all. I couldn't help feeling that others in similar circumstances might find some comfort too, if only they were able to share our experiences. I said to Steve that I really felt I should write about it.

At first he begged me not to do anything. He was afraid, understandably, that people would think we were either completely mad, or else that we'd made the whole thing up but, when things continued to happen and time was running into weeks, I broached the subject again. This was such a tremendous gift we'd been given; I was convinced we were meant to share it with others.

There is nothing special about Steve and me, so I knew that our experiences were, in all probability, not unique but as with Steve's reluctance to tell anyone else, I suspected that when this kind of thing happened, experiencers would likewise tend to keep it to themselves.

Firstly then, how was I going to contact these people and secondly, how could I persuade them to share their experiences with a complete stranger? Furthermore, would they trust that same stranger to recount their very personal stories in a book?

I have to admit, I found the prospect daunting and I really hadn't the first idea how or where to start. Like a lot of other good intentions, this one looked like being shelved.

The Beginning

Do you believe in coincidence? Personally I don't. I believe that everything happens for a reason. Sometimes things don't seem to make any sense at the time, then, looking back you can put all the pieces together and see why they happened.

*   *   *

We live in West Wales, right up in the mountains. Normal television reception is poor to say the least, except for Channel 5 and Steve was fed up watching Film on 5, so just before Christmas 2002 he subscribed to Sky Television, which opened up a whole new world (literally!) of programmes to us.

About a month after losing Sweep, we were watching TV one night, as usual. Steve was flicking through the channels when he came across two programmes on Living TV, 'Beyond', with James Van Praagh and 'Crossing Over', with John Edward. James and John are both Mediums. Both programmes, as you might expect, involve them contacting loved ones who have passed. I have a completely open mind when it comes to Mediums. As far as I'm concerned, as with everything, there are good and bad. The two programmes became almost compulsive viewing for us. In the light of what was happening in our own lives at the time, they seemed totally relevant.

Some weeks later, we turned on the TV one night, just in time to catch the beginning of Crossing Over. John Edward was introducing two people, whose names I didn't catch. He said they had written a fantastic book about After Death Communication with loved ones who have passed. I did catch the name of the book, which was 'Hello From Heaven'. John enthused about it so much that I felt I must read it, so the next day I went into our local bookshop and ordered it. I said it was a new book (!) but I had no idea who the author/s were. Within two weeks they rang to say it was in stock and waiting to be collected.

What an amazing book! I read it from cover to cover with hardly a break. Even more amazing was that on reading it again later for reference, I found that it was first published in 1995! So although it had been around for eight years, it had only now come to my notice, at the time when I needed to know how to proceed with my own project. It answered all my questions and I knew exactly what I needed to do next.

The co-authors of *Hello From Heaven*, Bill and Judy Guggenheim, researched their subject extensively for seven years. In that time they interviewed more than 2000 people to obtain 3300 accounts of After Death Communications (ADC's) with deceased loved ones. Their book is not only unique but gives an amazing insight into what happens when we depart this earthly life. Reading it was confirmation for me that I had to write about ADC's with animals.

The next step then was to contact people. The obvious thing to do was to write to the weekly dog papers. I faxed the same letter to two well-known papers and one printed it the same week. This produced a favourable response and some amazing experiences to add to our own. I waited several weeks but nothing appeared in the other paper. Eventually I wrote to Jane Lilley, writer of 'Living With Dogs' in *Dog World*. I know her column is widely read and respected. To my great delight, she not only devoted half of her column to my request but also included two of her own experiences in validation and featured the subject for several weeks afterwards.

What became evident was, that the ADC's being reported with animals, were similar in virtually every respect to those with people.

Contact Explained

In *Hello From Heaven*, Bill and Judy Guggenheim identify several main ways in which those that have passed make contact with us. According to their research, the most common of these are: sense (Sentient), sound (Auditory), smell (Olfactory), sight (Visual), touch (Tactile), dreams (Dream-State) and visions. The use of symbols (Symbolic) and physical phenomena are also quite common. Each ADC may contain just one or two elements, or a combination of several.

From all the accounts of animal ADC's which I've been given, departed pets make contact with us in exactly the same way as departed loved ones, using all of the means mentioned. In fact, the only means I haven't yet come across is by telephone. Somehow, I don't think that's likely; unless of course, someone out there has lost a parrot that wants to get in touch!

In order to better understand each form of contact, a brief explanation may be helpful.

* * *

Sense (Sentient). This is when the 'presence' of the departed loved one is felt. Each visit has a beginning and an end and experiencers have the distinct feeling that their loved one is with them, even though they may not be able to see them.

Sound (Auditory). Hearing a voice, or familiar noise. This can either be heard in the normal way, i.e. externally, through the ears; or internally, i.e. inside the head or the mind but originating from an outside source; as with telepathy.

Smell (Olfactory). Where the presence of a smell, fragrance, aroma, is noticed, which belongs unmistakeably to the one who has passed.

Sight (Visual). Where the deceased loved one makes either a full or partial appearance.

With a partial appearance they may be; only partly visible; wholly visible but not solid; or they may appear in, or as, a brilliant light.

With a full appearance, the whole body is seen, solid, as in life and always healed of any former illness or disability. In particular, these appearances generally give their experiencers great comfort and/or healing.

Dreams (Sleep-state). Easily distinguishable from ordinary dreams because they are more vivid, colourful and real. Also, details of events stay clearly in the minds of experiencers, even years afterwards. This is a very common kind of ADC, probably because the mind is more relaxed and open when asleep.

Similarly, contact of any kind may occur when you are just dozing, daydreaming, or on the point of sleeping or waking up. Again, the mind is relaxed and receptive.

Symbols (Symbolic). Butterflies (a symbol for the Resurrection) and moths; rainbows, feathers and flowers are all spirit signs. Birds, animals and even everyday objects can also be signs. Interpretation is up to the individual but when a sign appears, there is no mistaking that it is indeed a sign.

N.B. John Edward advises not to look too hard for signs, 'Because,' he says, 'In looking, we may miss the subtle sign that is the true message.'

Physical Phenomena. These include windows and doors opening or closing; objects moving; lights and all kinds of electrical devices being switched on or off; pictures moving and clocks and watches stopping.

There are other less common types of ADC's. These include:

Touch (Tactile). The experiencer feels actual physical contact in some way, from the departed loved one.

Visions. These may be external, i.e. outwardly seen with the eyes; or internal, i.e. in the mind. In either case they appear as brightly coloured films or slides, either floating in the air, or, as though the experiencer was looking through a screen.

ADC's that happen before the experiencer is aware of death

occurring. Proof that ADC's are not imagination, hallucinations, or grief-induced memories.

Shared ADC's. Where more than one person experiences contact simultaneously.

Evidential. When something is made known to you that you neither knew, nor had any way of knowing, beforehand; e.g. where something has been hidden.

*   *   *

For the purposes of this book, I feel that these are the relevant types of ADC. There are examples of all of them in the accounts that follow. *Hello From Heaven* contains several more types of ADC that I have omitted, such as those for protection and suicide intervention and also by way of the telephone! There seems to be no way in which contact cannot be established.

*   *   *

One other type of ADC that I have not included but perhaps should have, is the Out of Body ADC, something which I thought at first could not possibly be relevant to animals. There is one account however that made me think twice about that too!

At Rest

A reader wrote to the editor of his local paper, asking: *"Where shall I bury my dog?"*

We would say to that man that there are various places in which a dog may be buried. We are thinking now of a Setter whose coat was flame in the sunshine and who, so far as we are aware, never entertained a mean or unworthy thought. This particular Setter is buried beneath a cherry tree, under 4ft of garden loam and in its proper season the cherry tree strews petals on the green lawn of his grave.

Beneath a cherry tree, or an apple or any flowering shrub is an excellent place to bury a good dog. Beneath such trees, such shrubs, he slept in the drowsy summer or gnawed at a flaverous bone, or lifted his head to challenge some strange intruder. These are good places in life or death. Yet it is a small matter. For if the dog be well remembered, if sometimes he leaps through your dreams actual as in life, eyes kindling, laughing, begging, it matters not at all where that dog sleeps. On a hill where the wind is unrebuked, and the trees are roaring, or beside a stream he knew in puppyhood, or somewhere in the flatness of a pasture land where most exhilarating cattle graze. It is all one to the dog and all one to you and nothing is gained and nothing lost – if memory lives.

But there is one best place to bury a dog. If you bury him in this spot he will come to you when you call – come to you over the grim, dim frontiers of death, and down the well remembered path and to your side again. And though you call a dozen living dogs to heel they shall not growl at him, nor resent his coming for he belongs there. People may scoff at you who see no lightest blade of grass bent by his footfall, who hear no whimper; people who may never really have had a dog. Smile at them, for you shall know something that is hidden from them and that is well worth knowing – The one best place to bury a good dog is in the heart of his master.

(Condensed from *How Could I be Forgetting* by Ben Hur Lampman)

Judging by the wonderful response I had to my appeal for contributions to this book, there are many good dogs (and other pets) buried in the hearts of their masters. So, now we'll see how they continue to repay that love, even after they've departed this life. I'll begin with Sweep's story, because for us at least, that was the beginning of this chapter of our lives; when suddenly all things became possible.

*   *   *

I will lend to you for a while, a pup, God said,
For you to love him while he lives and mourn for him when he's dead.
Maybe for twelve or fourteen years, or maybe two or three
But will you, 'til I call him back, take care of him for me?
He'll bring his charms to gladden you and, (should his stay be brief),
You'll always have his memories as solace for your grief.
I cannot promise he will stay, since all from earth return
But there are lessons taught below I want this pup to learn.
I've looked the whole world over, in search of teachers true
And from the folk that crowd life's land, I have chosen you.
Now will you give him all your love nor think the labour vain,
Nor hate me when I come to take, my pup back again?
I fancied that I heard them say, "Dear Lord Thy Will be Done,"
For all the joys this pup will bring, the risk of grief we'll run.
We'll shelter him with tenderness; we'll love him while we may
And for the happiness we've known, forever grateful stay.
But, should you call him back much sooner than we've planned,
We'll brave the bitter grief that comes and try to understand.
If, by our love, we've managed, your wishes to achieve,
In memory of him we loved, to help us while we grieve,
When our faithful bundle departs this world of strife,
We'll have yet another pup and love him all his life.

Author Unknown

Sweep's Story

Wednesday 26th. February 2003 began much like any other day. After the usual round of dog-related chores and (some) housework in the morning I took Sweep for a walk and then set about stripping some of his coat in preparation for Crufts.

Sweep was my partner Steve's first Irish Wolfhound. I bred him; Steve chose him at two days old and named him Sweep because he used to squeak like Sooty's friend. By the time he was 22 months old he was almost 38″ to the shoulder and weighed fourteen and a half stone. His nature was as generous as his size. He was kindness itself and we both absolutely adored him but he was every inch Steve's dog. To say they idolised one another would not be putting it too strongly. Everyone who saw the two of them together remarked on the bond between them. Each morning before Steve left for work in the lorry, Sweep would sit on his knee for a cuddle and every afternoon he would listen for Steve's lorry coming up the lane and wait at the gate for him with his tail wagging wildly. Steve was immensely proud of him and really looking forward to showing him at Crufts.

I must admit, I got a bit carried away with the coat stripping. The more I took out the more needed to come out and eventually poor Sweep looked quite naked. When Steve got home from work and saw him he was not very impressed.

Some time later, I walked into the lounge to find projectile vomit all over the carpet but at that point I didn't know which dog was responsible because we had three living indoors, all of which had access to the lounge. I was cross because I'd vacuumed in there earlier. I cleaned the mess up, muttering something about 'B . . . dogs, why do I bother?'

About 6p.m., I took the outside dogs for their run on the field as usual and then went back to the house to fetch Sweep and the others for their run. Sweep stood on the patio with his head down. I don't ever remember seeing him standing like that before and when I called him he was reluctant to come. Eventually he followed me down the track to the field but didn't fly through the gate with the others as he usually did, just stayed near me the whole time. I took them all back up to the house and told Steve (who was in the garage tinkering with something mechanical) that I was going to phone the vet because something was the matter with Sweep. We realised then that it must have been him that had been sick, for whatever reason.

The receptionist at the vet's said to go straightaway as the surgery closed at 7pm. We managed to get there on the dot of seven but unfortunately, our usual vet, in whom we have great faith, was not on duty. His stand-in, after examining Sweep, taking his temperature (which was normal), checking his membranes (which I said were pale and she said were normal), diagnosed a stomach bug, gave him a painkiller, told us to take him home, not to feed him that night and to ring if we were worried.

On the way home we went through everything that he'd done that day. Was it the walk? Nothing unusual had happened while we were out. Had he picked up anything and eaten it? I was sure he hadn't and anyway he was never a scavenger – unlike his sisters. Was he stressed because I'd stripped so much of his coat out? I could only hope not on that score.

When we got home he wouldn't settle. We made him a huge squashy bed in the lounge (he always slept in the lounge on his quilt anyway) but each time he lay down he got up again straightaway. I told Steve to go to bed, as he had to be up for work at 6am. I said I would stay with Sweep but Steve said if we both went up then perhaps he would settle, so at 11.30pm we both went to bed.

I knew I wouldn't be able to sleep and kept listening for noises from the lounge, which is directly below our room. Every now and then I got out of bed to look down the stairs to see if Sweep was on his bed, which he was. After a while he began to cry every five minutes or so until at 3am I went down to him. He was off his bed and lying tightly curled up by the door. For a huge dog he looked so small.

I called his name but he didn't respond. His eyes were tiny and I realised that he was almost comatose. Steve had heard me trying to rouse him and asked from the top of the stairs if he was dead. I said not quite but I was going to ring the vet, at which point, to my amazement, Sweep got up and walked into the kitchen.

I took him outside to see if he needed to wee but he had a drink of water out of the bucket on the patio and then went back into the house. I rang the vet and said I was very worried as his condition had deteriorated. He had seemed to be in pain since we fetched him home and he was virtually comatose when I'd come downstairs to him. She said to get him back to the surgery and she would meet us there.

We arrived at 4am. This time he had blood tests as well as temperature (still normal) and all the usual. He was put on a drip and by 6am seemed to be a little brighter. The results of the blood tests showed that everything was 'normal'; including his liver, kidneys, pancreas etc. I mentioned again that I thought his membranes were pale but the vet said they were OK. She was convinced that it was a colicky stomach bug, said to take him home and she would ask our usual vet to do a house call on his way to surgery that morning.

He arrived at 8.30am. Having examined Sweep he said his membranes were pale (!) and he wasn't convinced that it wasn't a torsion we were dealing with. He took another blood sample and said to ring at 10am for the results. He also said that if nothing showed then he might have to do exploratory surgery to find out what was going on.

Steve rang at ten. The results showed that Sweep's white cell count was now up, apparently indicating a severe bacterial infection and Steve was to call at the surgery to fetch anti-inflammatorys and antibiotics.

By 10.20am Sweep was prone on the lounge floor and not responding to any stimuli. I rang the vets' again and said we were taking him straight in. We arrived at 11am and they were ready to operate almost immediately. We were there with him, as we always are with any of our dogs under anaesthetic.

When he was opened up, the first words the vet said were "Oh, poor dog." His abdomen was full of blood and it was a long while before the vet could find the source of the bleed. Eventually he found it was his liver. He said he could stitch him up, give him a transfusion, put him on a drip and see what happened. I asked what his chances were; realistically. The vet said "Less than 20%."

It was Steve's decision and he did the only thing he could and told the vet to let him go. That was probably the hardest thing he's ever had to do in his life to date but to his everlasting credit, he didn't hesitate. He said goodbye to his best friend and it broke his heart and mine too.

When we left the surgery Steve wanted to drive. Halfway home he broke down with heartrending sobbing, so I drove the rest of the way.

I'd lost dogs before; dogs that I loved and adored and whose loss hurt terribly but this was something else. Whether it was because it was so quick and so unexpected, or because Sweep was so young (22 months), or because he was such a huge presence in our lives, both physically and emotionally, I don't know; I just know it was an all-consuming pain, a physical ache that enveloped our whole bodies and rendered us numb and at the same time seeringly raw and sensitive.

So much guilt to cope with. Had I done anything to cause or contribute to his death?

Could we have done anything sooner or quicker to prevent it? Could the vets have done anything more? Had he been misdiagnosed in the first place? If he had, would he still be alive if he'd had the correct treatment or immediate surgery?

As we found out much later, when the biopsy results on the liver were known, there was nothing anyone could have done. What he had suffered was a liver torsion. According to our information, when this happens, (apparently it is very rare), one lobe of the liver twists and dies within minutes. The animal can live virtually normally for an indefinite period, as the other lobe then does all the work, until such time as the twisted lobe rights itself. At this point the blood starts to flow through the dead lobe and the animal haemorrhages. From the instant the lobe first twists, the animal is a walking time-bomb, literally waiting to die. There is little that can be done. It is deemed virtually inoperable. In any case and probably worst of all, there are no symptoms when it first happens, so by the time any kind of symptoms do appear it is definitely too late.

We got through the rest of that day somehow; I really don't know how. On auto-pilot I think. There were the other dogs to take care of, which we did. We tried to eat some dinner but neither of us was really hungry. We talked and tried to make some kind of sense of what had happened but we couldn't because there wasn't any kind of sense to be made of it. When we were totally exhausted we went to bed, quite late I think.

Friday 28th February

I was woken at 3.50am by the sound of intermittent moaning coming from downstairs. My first thoughts were 'Oh dear God, not another one please.' I got out of bed, put my dressing-gown on and went downstairs, to find Steve (who I hadn't realised wasn't in bed) lying on the floor where Sweep's bed had been. He was making the most dreadful moaning noise and I thought he was distressed, so put my hand on him to comfort him and told him to come back to bed. I thought he was awake but he had actually been asleep and was startled when I touched him and spoke to him. He didn't know where he was or what he was doing and was extremely shaken. Eventually he managed to get up and he said he had been dreaming.

We went back upstairs and got into bed and he began to tell me about the 'dream'. He said it seemed so real. In the 'dream', Emma, an acquaintance of ours in another breed, had appeared to Steve.

I should explain at this point, that Emma died just before Christmas, 2002. She was in her mid-thirties, happy and healthy and died completely unexpectedly in her sleep. We often spoke to her and her husband at shows and had become quite friendly with them, so her death had been quite a shock to us as well.

When Emma appeared to Steve, she said 'I've always wanted a Wolfhound, can I look after him (Sweep) for you?'

Steve said 'No, he's mine.'

Emma said 'I'll look after him till you come for him.'

Steve said 'No, you can't have him.'

Emma said 'I have to take him now, you have to let him go.'

It was at this point, unfortunately, that I disturbed Steve, not realising that he was not awake.

When he'd finished telling me what had happened, Steve asked me if I thought it was just a dream. I said no I didn't. It seemed to be much more than that but at that point neither of us had any idea what.

*   *   *

This wasn't the first time something 'unusual', for want of a better word, had happened to either of us.

When I first moved to Wales, in 1998, I bought a large house, part of which dated back to Victorian times, the rest a later extension. There were three bedrooms and mine was in the old part of the house. About the third night after moving in, I 'dreamt' that a ghost was pinning me to the bed and trying to suffocate me. I was struggling for breath and thought I was going to die. Suddenly, in the 'dream', I thought, 'God will save me', at which point the ghost immediately let go and vanished.

I woke up in a cold sweat and quite shaken but fortunately I'm not the sort of person who (usually) worries about dreams, so just put it down to being in a new house. I must admit though, that I was still quite shaken for the next couple of days and couldn't really understand why. I didn't tell anyone about the dream, not even when I spoke to my son on the phone.

A month or two later, two friends of mine from the Midlands, Val and Pam, came to stay; their first visit since I'd moved. Pam is quite a nervous person. She keeps all the doors and windows of her house locked, even when she's at home, even in the middle of summer. So that she'd feel safer, I'd put her in the middle bedroom, so she'd got me on one side and Val on the other. Pam's room, like mine, was in the old part of the house, whilst Val's was in the new extension.

The first morning I asked them both if they'd had a good night and slept well, as you do. Val said great but Pam said awful. When I asked why, she said she'd had a really bad dream. Apparently a ghost had pinned her to the bed and tried to strangle her! I didn't breathe a word about my own dream because I knew if I did I wouldn't see her for dust, then or ever again and I've never told her to this day.

One other 'dream' I had at the same house, some months later, was about a North American Indian with beautiful long, jet-black hair. He stood behind me and yet I could see the back of his head in front of me. He had his arm around my shoulder but not quite touching and when I sat, he sat and at the same time moved closer so that his arm was then firmly around my shoulder. I couldn't see his face but his presence was so comforting.

When I woke I felt totally calm and reassured. The 'dream' was so vivid that it stayed fresh and clear in my mind for days afterwards and even now, thinking back, I can still remember it clearly. I believe that this North American Indian is my spirit guide. (I did tell my son about this one. His interpretation of this was, that the Indian being behind me and yet me seeing the back of him in front of me, was like eternity and being surrounded with love and protection. Which I have to admit, is a pretty good interpretation as far as I'm concerned!)

About twelve months later, Steve moved in with me. I didn't tell him anything about the 'dreams'; in fact they had been forgotten really. The only one who did know by this time was my son.

*   *   *

Steve didn't like the house much; he thought it had an 'odd' feel to it. One evening, not long after he'd moved in, he went upstairs and I heard such a commotion that I went to see what was happening. When I asked him what was going on he said something had tried to push him down the stairs!

A few weeks after that, he was sitting in the lounge one night and he called through to the kitchen, 'Did your mother have something wrong with her chest?'

My mum had died the previous year, not long after I'd moved into the house. She'd never been there. Steve had never met her. He knew she had died but I'd never told him anything about her. I called back and said 'Yes, she had angina, why?' He called back, 'Because she's here with me now and she's holding her chest.'

*   *   *

So, knowing the kind of things that had happened in the past, I was fairly sure that what Steve had experienced the night of Sweep's death was not just a dream but something far more significant.

Saturday 1ˢᵗ March

I woke up at 4am. Steve started sobbing and talking to Sweep in his sleep. This time I didn't wake him.

Our bed is directly under the Velux window in our bedroom. I looked up through the Velux while Steve was still 'dreaming'. The sky was clear and full of stars. As I looked up, I asked in my head 'Are you there Sweep?' At that very instant, the brightest, fastest shooting star I've ever seen in my life, shot vertically from the centre of the Velux.

Steve woke from his 'dream' at 4.15am. He realised I was awake and apologised for waking me. I said he hadn't, I was already awake and asked him what he had been dreaming about. He said he had been holding Sweep, somewhere very green but he didn't feel that he should look around. I told him about the shooting star and he looked up through the Velux and said, 'But it's cloudy'. I looked up and sure enough there wasn't a star to be seen.

Sweep's registered name included the song title 'Smoke On The Water'. I said perhaps we should think of him now as 'Spirit In The Sky', which Steve thought was a nice idea. We eventually went back to sleep.

The next morning, Steve went out in the car. Before he got to the end of our road, 'Spirit In The Sky' was playing on the car radio.

Sunday 2ⁿᵈ March

4.15am. I was woken by Steve talking in his sleep. He woke up sobbing and I asked what he had been 'dreaming'. He said someone had brought Sweep today but he couldn't see who it was. He was aware of another dog there as well.

When we got up that morning, I went downstairs and heard a thud in the kitchen. When I opened the kitchen door, our old Wolfhound, Molly, was lying on the floor unable to get up. I tried to lift her but she was too heavy so I shouted Steve to come quickly. I think she must have slipped as she'd tried to stand up and she'd frightened herself. She seemed alright when we got her to her feet, just a bit shaky – not half as shaky as we were in our heightened emotional state. It was all beginning to seem just a bit too much.

At the same time, there appeared to be a pattern emerging and I thought I'd better start recording things in the diary as they happened, rather than relying on memory.

Monday 3ʳᵈ March

We have a Teasmade on the bedside table and the clock is quite easy to read because it has an orangey sort of light over it. I woke up, looked at the clock and thought it said 5am. I felt disappointed because I thought Sweep wasn't coming. I went back to sleep, woke again, looked at the clock and it said 2.05am. I thought I must be so tired I'd obviously misread it the first time.

I went back to sleep and woke again at 4.15am., thinking 'You're late today Sweep.' Straight away, Steve started mumbling in his sleep. When he woke I asked him to tell me what he'd 'dreamt'.

He said he'd been with Sweep. They were walking on what felt like sand. There was no sea or sky. Steve didn't think he had shoes on because he could feel the sand under his feet. He was telling Sweep how special he is.

He said their meetings usually end with Sweep stretching and fading. He feels Sweep decides when it's time to go.

*   *   *

Later that morning, I was in the kitchen and Molly was lying on her bed. Suddenly she sat up, looked at the doorway next to where I was standing and gave a warning bark. She's getting a bit crotchety in her old age and will often warn the others off if they get near her bed. This time there were no other (!) dogs indoors, or about to come indoors.

Tuesday 4th March

The same thing happened with the bedside clock as happened last night. I woke; looked at the clock, read it as 5am and thought again that Sweep wasn't coming today. I went back to sleep and was woken by Steve muttering. When I looked at the clock it was 4.20am. I smiled to myself and thought 'He's here.'

By now, although I always want Sweep to stay as long as possible, I'm also impatient for Steve to wake so that I can ask him what's happened and I'm beginning to ask for more details.

When he woke, he said that this time, Sweep had poked him on the leg to get his attention. He was standing four square, in show pose, head up, looking beautifully groomed, sleek and muscled, with his coat shining and rippling. He turned his head to look at Steve and Steve was conscious of his brown eyes. He was surrounded by a bright light. As usual, he just faded when it was time to go.

Each time Steve had one of these 'dreams', which by now we were referring to as 'visits', he woke with a tremendous headache, which he describes as being like a hangover (I wouldn't know about that!). He said it seemed to centre on a point about two inches above the middle of his forehead. I remembered reading about Chakras some time ago and had a suspicion this might be one. Chakras are the main energy centres of the spiritual body.

Later that morning, after Steve had gone to work, I looked in *Your Healing Power* by Jack Angelo. It says:

'The Crown Chakra. On the top of the head. This is the input centre for spiritual energies. It provides a direct link with the Source and deals with all issues of spirituality. At a physical level, it is linked to the pineal gland (the light detector). Its energies also affect the brain and the rest of the body.

When in a state of balance, the crown chakra vibrates to the colour violet.'

*   *   *

Now I felt we were getting somewhere!

Wednesday 5th March

Wednesday 5th March

I was woken from my own dream by Steve talking to Sweep. I looked at the clock and this time it really was 5am. I managed to catch the odd word here and there. I heard Steve say 'Love you Sweep', 'Good boy Sweep' and then after a long conversation, 'See you later Sweep, good boy.'

Steve took two enormous deep breaths and then shook, as if he was walking in his sleep. He turned over and woke up. He had a terrific headache again.

He said he had to call Sweep to him today. He had been bounding around playing. His coat was immaculate and gleaming. Steve had to attract his attention and was conscious of someone being with him but he couldn't see who it was. It was as though they were just 'out of frame'. Everywhere was green and it felt like grass underfoot. (Whenever he describes colours in these visits, he always says that they are extremely bright and vivid; unlike any colours in this life.) Steve told Sweep that he wanted to be with him and at that point he felt the 'out of frame' figure step closer. Eventually Sweep ran off.

While Steve is having his 'visits' with Sweep, I talk to Sweep in my head. In August 2002, I had had to say goodbye to Sweep's grandma, Jenna. She was such a character, a true Alpha bitch and also very pretty, being a striking red with a wheaten top coat. I loved her dearly but sadly she had an autoimmune condition that she'd battled with for three years. It affected the bridge of her nose, which was constantly raw and bleeding and her hind feet. Although I'd tried every possible remedy, including prayer, nothing worked for long and eventually I made the decision to let her go to the Rainbow Bridge, at just seven years old. I asked Sweep if he could find Grandma Jenna and bring her with him, so that I could see that she is alright and happy too, (if she'd come that is – knowing Jenna she'd say she couldn't be bothered!) I didn't mention this to Steve.

Thursday 6th March

Sweep didn't come. We were both disappointed but hoped it was because we'd had to be up before 4.30am and Sweep hadn't had time to come through.

Friday 7th March

No Sweep again today. We were up early again, to take Steve's Danes to Crufts. I hadn't wanted to go but Steve said he felt he should.

Saturday 8th March

We were up early again and Sweep hadn't been. Steve said he didn't think he would come any more. Today was the day we'd been dreading. It was Hound day at Crufts and the day Steve had been looking forward to so much with Sweep. I really didn't want to go but Steve said he had to go and face the other Wolfhound people and get it over with. If he didn't go today he might not be able to face them at the Wolfhound Club Show.

He was sure that when Sweep had shown him his beautiful, immaculately groomed coat and stood so proudly in show stance, it was because he'd wanted us to go to Crufts as planned and I wasn't about to argue with that.

So we went and we actually had a brilliant day under the circumstances. Everyone was so kind and thoughtful. Many of them of course have been in exactly the same position, having lost much-loved hounds. It was very hard being there without Sweep but we were glad we'd done it after all.

*   *   *

Sweep sitting in the garden. Age 4 months.

Sweep, age 5 months, posing in the garden.

Sweep, age 7 months, in the garden, (Molly in background).

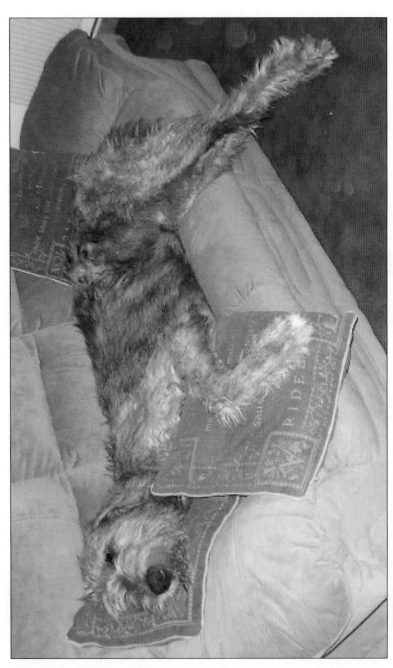

Sweep age 20 months. Taken Christmas Day – sleeping off his Christmas dinner.

Sweep by the gate, age 1 year, 2 months.

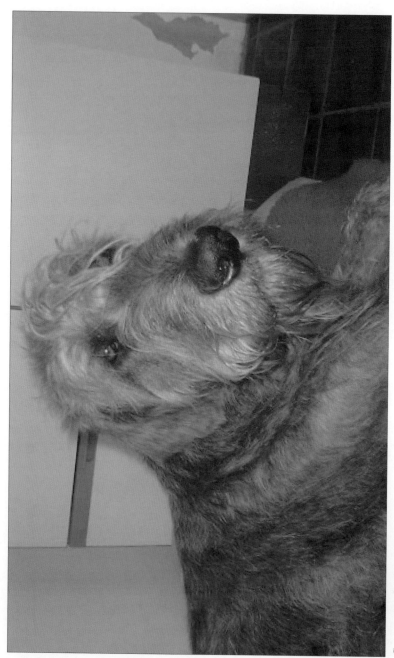

Sweep in the kitchen.

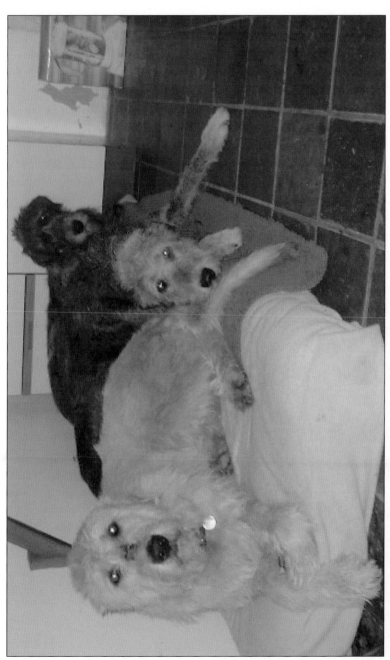

Jenna in the kitchen with Molly & Mole. N.B. Jenna's nose.

Sweep ready for his holidays!

Photo by Carol Ann Johnson

Sweep age 17 months. Taken at Belfast when he won his Reserve C.C.

Sweep in his favourite place, on Steve's knee.

Sweep enjoying the snow, three weeks before he died.

Phantom and Lucy. See page 118.

Phantom saying Goodbye. See page 119.

Spirit Dog Fidget. See page 125.

Spirit Dog Hunter. See page 125.

Steve had decided that he needed to have another male Wolfhound, not to replace Sweep, that would be impossible but to try to fill part of the enormous hole that he had in his heart. While we were at Crufts we were offered a young dog from Ireland, whose breeding we liked. We made arrangements to go across to see him the following weekend.

Sunday 9th March

5.10am. I woke to hear Steve talking to Sweep. What a joy! He had come again after all. I have to lie really still while this is happening so that I don't wake Steve and I'm straining my ears trying to catch any words that I can make sense of. I heard him telling Sweep that we were going to Ireland next weekend.

Steve woke up sobbing with the usual, (by now), very bad headache.

He said he had been dreaming about a dog show. The dream was in black and white but gradually it turned to colour. The ground was green and the background was a bright light (but not white). He described it as – 'as though I was looking through a television screen or frame'. Sweep trotted up into the frame with the shadow of another dog behind. Then he trotted away out of frame. Steve called after him 'Don't go yet.' Sweep came back – with Jenna! She sat down in front of Steve and held her paw up to him, just as he'd taught her to do in this life. Her nose and feet were healed and her coat was groomed and shining.

Eventually they both started playing and then ran off and faded.

(Of course I cried when Steve told me, I cried when I wrote it and I've cried every time I've read it, which must be dozens of times by now; it just makes me so happy.)

*   *   *

Later that morning, Steve was getting breakfast ready while I did the dogs. He was talking to Sweep in his head and asked him what he should call the new puppy if we brought him home from Ireland.

He'd walked into the lounge at this point and looked at the shelf above the television. He had the radio on as usual and just as his eyes rested on the bottle of Bailey's Irish Cream on the shelf, there was a request on the radio for a Mr. & Mrs. Bailey; so it seemed that Sweep had chosen 'Bailey' as the name!

Wednesday 12ᵗʰ March

Sweep's first visit since Sunday. I didn't wake up for this one, so I don't know what time it was, except that it was before the alarm went off at 6am.

Steve said Sweep walked up to him and they walked together on a green surface. He told Sweep that Chance (one of the Danes) is going to Ireland this weekend when we go to see the puppy. There was no-one with him this time and no other dogs and he had his 'at home' coat.

Steve woke with the usual headache and tiredness but wasn't upset this time.

Saturday 15ᵗʰ March

We took Chance (the Dane bitch) to Ireland and came home with a very outgoing nine-month old Irish Wolfhound dog puppy – who will be called 'Bailey'; as per Sweep's instructions!

Wednesday 19ᵗʰ March

Sweep came again today. I woke to hear Steve talking quite clearly to him. He was telling him about Bailey and asking if his name was right. Time 4.55a.m.

Steve cried when he woke up and said he had a really bad headache. He said everywhere was a light green, lighter than before. Sweep had trotted up to him and nudged him, then rubbed his head on him. Steve says he always knows when he's getting ready to go because he has a certain look on his face and he gets fidgety. When he went this time, he trotted off and faded. He was on his own today.

Saturday 22*nd* March

Steve collected Sweep's ashes from the vet. They are in a dark brown mahogany casket and now live on the sideboard in the lounge with a photograph of Sweep resting against them.

Wednesday 26*th* March

Steve put the computer on and got Emma's* website up. Steve had visited her website several times before but for some reason had never seen her photo album. This time he did; only to find a picture of Emma with her dog – named 'Bailey'!

Saturday 29*th* March

I woke at 4a.m., thinking – 'Where are you Sweep? You haven't been to see us for ages, are you going to come and say hello? How are you? Are you OK?

At 4.40a.m., Steve started muttering. I heard him say, 'Hello, where have you been?' I heard him mention Sweep's name every so often and Bailey's. The conversation lasted until 4.50am and then I heard him say 'Go on then. Bye Sweepie.'

The pattern was the same when he woke up; two or three really deep breaths, shaking and then crying.

He said this time, when Sweep appeared, he was lying down in a silver/white light. He (Steve) sensed someone was with him although he couldn't see them. He said it felt like sand underfoot, which he was aware of because he didn't have any shoes on.

* Who came to Steve the first night after Sweep died.

Sweeps' eyes were bright and his coat was good. He kept rubbing against Steve and poking him with a front leg. (Steve had jumped several times while he was asleep – I had wondered why). When it was time to go, Sweep trotted away and back again, then away and faded. Steve said it all felt very real this time.

Friday 4ᵗʰ April

Strange visit from Sweep. Strange time too. 0.45a.m. I wasn't asleep. Steve started muttering. I couldn't make out any words at all. The visit only lasted 4–5 minutes. Steve took three deep breaths and was awake. He said Sweep was in like a fog or mist. He felt as though they had to speak very quietly, as if they were doing something they shouldn't. There was no contact at all, Sweep faded in through the mist and faded out when he went.

* * *

When Steve was leaving for work at 6.20am, he said Sweep's visit last night (or this morning), had been like watching a TV that wasn't tuned in properly. It was as if Steve had 'connected' too early and Sweep hadn't come through properly.

Saturday 5ᵗʰ April

The Irish Wolfhound Club Championship Show. This was the one Steve had been dreading and neither of us really enjoyed it.

Before Sweep died, Steve had been looking forward so much to this show. He knew Sweep was sure to win the height cup. Unfortunately fate decreed otherwise. Despite trying very hard all day to put a brave face on it, we were both glad when it was over.

Wednesday 9th April

I 'spoke' to Sweep and asked him to come & visit but he didn't come today.

Thursday 10th April

Sweep came today. 5a.m. I woke to Steve's muttering, most of which was quite clear. I heard him say, 'Where have you been? I've missed you.' – 'Wendy misses you too. You've been away too long'. He told him about the show. I knew the visit was about to end when I heard him say 'Bye then Sweepie, don't stay away so long next time.'

He woke sobbing with the usual headache. He said he had been dreaming and called to Sweep who came trotting up to him in a grey light, which turned to a silvery white light. There was no-one with him. He poked Steve two or three times, (again, Steve had jumped in his sleep). Steve said he could feel his coat when he stroked him and that he looked happy and well. He became restless when it was time to go, then he trotted off. The visit lasted 7 or 8 minutes.

Monday 19th May

I decided that today was the day to get started on Sweeps' book, which is going to be called 'Over The Rainbow Bridge'. I faxed a letter to both of the dog papers asking if they would print it on their letters page.

Went shopping with Steve in the afternoon and saw a double rainbow* on the way home while I was telling Steve what I'd done.

---

* Took that to mean that Sweep approves of the book's title!

Tuesday 20ᵗʰ May

Started putting Sweeps' book onto the computer.

Had a letter from my friend Sue, thanking me for her birthday present. Very newsy letter as I hadn't heard from her for ages. She said she'd been away for a few days, staying with a friend in Leicestershire. While she was there she went to the friend's art class with her. Said it was great, – she'd been learning how to paint rainbows! (Definitely think I've got the title right.)

Wednesday 21ˢᵗ May

Sweep came last night. Steve had been upset yesterday when he read what I'd written. It brought it all back for him.

Before I went to sleep I'd 'asked' Sweep to come and see Steve because he needed him. I woke just before 2.30am to hear Steve muttering. I heard him say Sweep's name, 'I've missed you so much', 'Beautiful boy', then, 'Bye bye Sweepie' twice when he went. He sounded so sad.

It was the usual pattern on waking, two deep breaths, shaking, headache (& sobbing). Steve said he called Sweep and he appeared as a see-through shadow, which became clearer. He was in a white light and Steve hugged him. Sweep nudged him and rubbed against his legs. Steve said he looked beautiful. When it was time to go he got fidgety, licked Steve's face, then trotted off, came back a little way and then trotted off again and faded.

Monday 14ᵗʰ July

Sweep came last night. I woke at 2.40am to hear Steve muttering. It was unclear at first but I thought it must be Sweep. Then I heard Steve say 'Bailey', then Bozo's* name and 'shows are not the same'.

---

* Bozo is Jenna's son. He came back to live with us in June this year, 2003, after his owners split up. Although he is Sweep's Uncle, they had never met.

After a lengthy talk, Steve started wriggling about and giggling. He said 'Ooh, slurpy kisses'; more giggles and wriggling, then 'Big slurpy kisses'.* (I was beginning to wonder if it was Sweep he was talking to!) After a while the conversation went quiet. Steve took two deep breaths and woke up crying. The visit had lasted ten minutes.

Steve said Sweep seemed to appear at the side of the bed and he turned over to see him standing there. (This in itself was quite strange because, in real life, we have a spiral staircase which would be virtually impossible for a Wolfhound to climb – never mind descend, apart from which, we never allow dogs in the bedroom. As much as we love the dogs, it's just something that we choose not to do; so in real life this situation would never have happened.) We had been to a barbecue with some friends of ours, also with Wolfhounds, on the preceding Saturday, (12ᵗʰ July) and this subject had come up in conversation. I had made a point of saying that we *never* allow dogs in the bedroom. Obviously, Sweep was making the point that *he* could now go wherever he chose to!

Steve said that after he turned over and saw Sweep, they went outside. It was all green, with no sky and it felt as if they were on grass. Sweep was bounding about and very playful. His eyes were crystal clear. Steve was hugging him and could feel him as if he was real. After a while he ran off and Steve called him back. He came instantly but was very fidgety, as if he had to go. Eventually he trotted off.

Steve said that this time, when he woke up, apart from the usual headache, he felt much better physically. All his usual aches and pains had gone. He suffers with a bad back and sore legs and ankles but after this 'visit', all the discomfort was gone. He said it felt as if he had been given healing.

---

* I asked him about the slurpy kisses and the wriggling and giggling. He said Sweep was licking his feet! Sounds plausible. When Sweep was still with us in this life, he used to love to get his tongue between Steve's bare toes. He'd slurp away for ages and Steve would be wriggling about and laughing. There's no accounting for taste.

Sunday 7th September 2003

After a long absence, Sweep came again today. Just after 5am, I was woken by Steve mumbling in his sleep. I wasn't sure at first that it was Sweep, because the mumbling was very faint and incomprehensible. Gradually it got louder and clearer and then I heard Steve say 'I miss you' and knew it was definitely Sweep. He said 'Where have you been? Never a day goes by when I don't miss you. – Bozo's here; he's back. Bozo's come back.' (I wondered why he was telling Sweep that again, as he never met him.) Steve jumped several times and kept saying 'Sweepie! – Sweepie! – Sweepie!, at intervals and then started giggling.

The conversation lasted till 5.15am and then I couldn't quite make out the words but Steve sounded anxious. Eventually I heard him say 'Alright then, bye.' He went very quiet and still, took two deep breaths, shook quite violently and woke up crying, with a headache.

I touched him to comfort him and let him know I was awake and he said 'Sweepie's been again.' I said 'I know.' I told him how long it had lasted and asked him to tell me what he could remember.

The first thing he said was that Sweep had Jenna with him. Sweep appeared first as a shadow, which gradually got clearer and denser until it was just like Sweep in this life. Then Jenna appeared in the same way. Steve said Sweep was poking him and nudging and pushing his head into him, (hence the jumping and giggling), while Jenna just stood back a little, wagging her tail. Both seemed happy and their coats were gleaming and well-groomed. Jenna's nose and feet were perfectly healthy. It was Jenna (Bozo's mum) that Steve had been telling about Bozo coming back. Steve also said that he was telling Sweep about our latest visit to Ireland but I hadn't heard anything that I could relate to that.

Steve said the surroundings this time were like a feeling of space and although Sweep and Jenna were clearly visible in a bright light, the rest of the surroundings were dark. He couldn't feel anything underfoot or sense anything else around, just space.

Eventually they both started playing together and moved away from Steve. He called them back and they came but then carried on playing and moved away again until they gradually faded back to shadows and disappeared.

Steve said he felt full of energy after this visit and again, all his usual aches and pains had gone.

*   *   *

Up to the time of writing, this has been the last visit from Sweep. We have drawn so much comfort from the time he has spent with us since his passing. Steve says that after all the visits it's as if he has been 'empowered'. Although he feels drained emotionally, he feels almost electrically charged with energy and as if he has been given healing for his various aches and pains. For me, the feeling immediately after a visit is one of complete calmness and knowing. I have no fear whatever about leaving this earthly life. We both feel truly privileged to have been given this insight into 'life' on the other side.

Your Stories

The accounts that follow are from the people who contacted me, by letter, e-mail and telephone, following my appeal for contributions to this book.

Each is printed in good faith that it is a true and representative account of events. Nothing has been added for dramatic effect.

Where the experiencers telephoned me, I made notes as they spoke and typed the notes up immediately afterwards, while the conversation was fresh in my mind. I hope and trust that I have been accurate in my interpretation.

In the case of letters and e-mails; they have been reproduced in the way in which they were written, i.e., using the writer's own words; occasionally interspersed with my own thoughts or comments but never to alter the facts.

The majority of names have been altered to protect privacy but every account is from a genuine experiencer. I have all names and addresses/e-mail addresses, or contact numbers on file.

Except where stated, to the best of my knowledge the experiencers are unconnected, so it is highly unlikely that they will have conferred in any way. What will become apparent is the similarity in detail, where different experiencers have had the same type of ADC.

I hope that you, the reader, will be as enthralled, amazed and moved as I have been.

*   *   *

I have not attempted to categorize the accounts. I will leave it to you, the reader, to decide into which type of ADC category they fit. Several that I have left until towards the end, raise issues that I hope to expand on in a future book.

The Cross-Stitch Samoyed

Barbara telephoned.

About four or five years ago, a friend of Barbara's used to take her to dog shows but would never accept any payment. As a thankyou, Barbara decided to make her a cross-stitch picture of a Samoyed, as this was her favourite breed. She found a picture of what she thought was a very handsome Samoyed and although she realised it was quite probably a show dog, she was unable to find out either its name or its identity.

The night she started work on the picture, Barbara's Akita and her daughter's Giant Schnauzer were in the room with her. She was suddenly aware that they were both wagging their tails and when she looked up, there standing between them was the Samoyed from the picture! Barbara says he had the distinctive 'Sammy' grin on his face. Neither of the other dogs seemed at all worried by his presence, just accepted him as part of the family.

It took Barbara about four or five evenings to complete the picture and each evening the Samoyed would appear and stay while she worked. After the picture was completed she never saw him again.

*   *   *

Another animal to visit Barbara is her Siamese cat, which died two years ago. He lived to a ripe old age and was very vocal. Barbara still hears him calling now and then.

Charlotte

Janice telephoned.

Charlotte was Janice's Bull Terrier bitch. She was eight and a half years old when she had to be put to sleep due to kidney failure. According to Janice, Charlotte was basically lazy. She would spend a great deal of time in her bed in Janice's bedroom but each night, at 10pm prompt, she would come downstairs for her supper.

The family hadn't long moved house and as they were decorating there were no carpets in the upstairs rooms, or on the staircase. Charlotte's nails could be heard quite clearly, clacking across the bedroom floor and then all the way down the stairs, en-route to the kitchen. Sometimes, after she'd gone upstairs to bed during the day, the door of the bedroom would close behind her, shutting her in. At suppertime, if this had happened, Charlotte would scratch at the bedroom door until someone went up to let her out.

Janice had two other dogs at the time, Hungarian Pulis, named Holly and Chloe. When Holly arrived Charlotte was four years old and she 'adopted' her, the two becoming great friends. When Charlotte appeared for supper, Holly would wag her tail to greet her. Charlotte and Chloe on the other hand, never hit it off. Charlotte would occasionally snap at Chloe and she in turn would exit the kitchen and run and hide when she knew Charlotte was due to make an appearance.

Janice didn't realise at first that Charlotte was ill. She was looking at photos of the dogs one day, just after they'd moved, when she suddenly noticed that Charlotte had dropped about half her normal bodyweight. She lost no time in getting her to the vet and he diagnosed kidney failure. Charlotte's condition gradually worsened and Janice asked her vet if, when the time came, he would put Charlotte to sleep at home in her own bed. He said that of course he would.

In the early hours of April 1st 1999, Janice knew that the time had come to let her go. The vet arrived at 5.30am. At 5.50am, Charlotte was put to sleep in her own bed in Janice's bedroom. So that the neighbours wouldn't see and be upset, Janice and her daughter buried Charlotte in their back garden under cover of darkness.

Some hours later, Janice's daughter noticed that one of the clocks had stopped. When they looked around the house, every single clock had stopped – at 5.50am. They were left unaltered. Twenty-four hours later, of their own accord, every one started working again; with the exception of the landing clock, which has never worked since and still shows the time at 5.50.

Two nights after Charlotte was put to sleep, Janice was woken by the sound of nails on the floorboards of the bedroom. She immediately thought 'That's Charlotte' and sat up to see Charlotte walk round the foot of the bed and along the side of the bed towards her, slowly wagging her tail as she did so. Then she disappeared.

Janice woke her partner to tell him she'd just seen Charlotte but he said she must have dreamt it and she thought he must be right.

The next night, Janice and her daughter were sitting downstairs when they heard the familiar sound of nails on the floorboards above and then descending the stairs. This happened every night for about three weeks. Sometimes it would be accompanied by scratching at the bedroom door, which would continue for several minutes, until Janice would say 'I'll have to go and let her out' and would go up, open the bedroom door and the scratching would stop.

Even Janice's partner had to admit that he could hear it too! Holly (Puli) would get terribly excited and wag her tail to greet her friend. Chloe would still exit the kitchen at 10pm every night and hide in the living-room.

One night when Janice's son had popped in for a visit he heard the nails on the floorboards above. 'What's that?' he asked and was told that it was Charlotte visiting. Janice says he stood with his head up the chimney trying to hear it more clearly!

During the latter part of Charlotte's illness, she had a distinctive smell about her, (which often seems to accompany this kind of condition). Janice says that on every occasion when Charlotte was heard, the smell was quite clearly present.

*   *   *

Janice had always had a 'Bully' about and because she couldn't bear to be without one, she arranged to see a puppy but wasn't allowed to visit her until she was three weeks old. When she did get to see her, she found out that she had been born the night that Charlotte was put to sleep. From the time that Janice saw the puppy, Charlotte's visits stopped, except for one other occasion.

One day, Janice and her daughter were indoors, when Holly became really excited, running back and forth to the patio door, as if to get them to follow her. Janice's daughter said 'What's the matter, what do you want? I don't understand.' With that, Holly ran over to where Charlotte's photo hung on the wall, jumped up and down in front of it and barked, then ran back to the patio door and barked, asking to be let out.

Once outside, she ran to a puddle of water which had 'appeared' on the patio slabs, sniffed at it, then ran about the garden wagging her tail, returning frequently to sniff the puddle again. Janice and her daughter are firmly convinced that it was Charlotte; this time returning to say goodbye to her friend Holly.

Brandy & Lisa

(June's own words – from her letter)

I have owned dogs since the age of nine years old and am now sixty-three. I am at the moment grieving my latest favourite and did everything I could for him, as he did for me. Personally, I have always kept these things to myself, mindful of being (thought) deranged in grief but now feel able to share my experiences in the open.

In those years, I have had two dogs that have shown themselves after death. The first was a Corgi cross, named Brandy, that I owned in the early 1960's before we started a family. She grew up with our children so it was a busy time. This dog was telepathic. She told me when my husband was about to arrive home from work so that I could get his dinner on the table accurately before he walked in the door. She told me the cat was in dire trouble after being run over and led me to him. When left with my parents when we went on holiday, every time I thought of her, my mother could give me the time I did it. She even told me my parents were on their way to see us when they were up to their knees in floodwater to see if we were alright. Brandy swam against the current with me, on her insistence that we went out. I cannot describe how I felt when the time came to give her sleep. This was the dog that I saw in the clouds, frolicking, for at least three months after her death. It never occurred to me that anyone else could witness that. I have searched the clouds since for other dogs and found nothing. I have to say I found it most comforting to see her in this way.

The next was a Flat-Coated Retriever, named Lisa. I had her as a young working dog (guide dog). She had to retire due to slipped discs in her back and she had a mini nervous breakdown in her new home with me. She opened up a whole new world to me, in training to keep her mind occupied and to accept me as a competent new owner.

In later life I found her in severe pain and took her to the vet, never dreaming I should return home without her. It was a very traumatic time and I was in shock.

After her death, on our favourite walk by the river, I saw her lying in the water in the same place every time. It upset me to see her and I avoided the area with my other dog for some time. Gradually I returned to walk my other dog and even got on speaking terms with Lisa in her position in the water.

Then we moved away from the area and many months passed before I found myself walking my dogs in the same place when I was revisiting the area. There was Lisa in the same position, in the exact spot I always saw her in the past. Only this time, she moved. I felt faint and sick. Someone nearby saw me and came to help. It was the owner of the dog in the water. To this day I have never seen Lisa again and like to think she re-lives in this dog. Flat-Coated Retrievers are uncommon in this area.

I have owned very special once-in-a-lifetime dogs since and have had no feedback from them, though I have searched the clouds, looked for them on walks and talked to them in my grief, with no response. I can only say that, with these dogs, I had a chance to say a proper farewell and prepare them for a long sleep.

*   *   *

After reading June's letter, I wrote to her to ask if she could tell me anymore about the time/s when she saw Brandy in the clouds. Here is what she wrote back to me:

*   *   *

You ask about Brandy who died in 1979 but I can remember it as if it were yesterday.

I had taken her to the vet in the evening to be put to sleep, as she was failing fast. He actually drove from his home to the surgery to do it. As I have said before, this dog was telepathic and I worried about her knowing what I was going to do to her and how she felt about it.

The next morning, after a tearful night, I pulled back the bedroom curtains and stared blankly out of the window, wondering how I was going to face the day without her and wondering about how the children were going to cope with her passing.

Brandy had reached the grand age of sixteen, so I suppose she just wore out but I had not prepared myself for the end.

There she was in the sky, running past the window and looking in as if to say, 'Everything is fine and I am happy here'. The relief was enormous. What I was looking at was a cloud travelling over the sky in the very shape of her to the tip of her tail at first. The movement of the cloud depicted her legs running along but as it went, her form elongated and slowly distorted, until I could no longer recognise the shape any more.

How long the image lasted is difficult to say, it seemed a long time but was probably only, at the most, half a minute. It was a cloudy day and the wind was moving the clouds along but there were breaks in the clouds with clear sky in between. After that experience, I looked for her there often, sometimes I saw her but most often I didn't but I do know I saw her at intervals over the next three months or so. Possibly the weather changed as well and that type of cloud was not about.

I have to say that at the time, I managed an allotment and had two children. I was probably more aware of the weather forecast than most people and did tend to search the sky automatically for black rainclouds before hanging the washing out or watering the vegetables. It has remained with me and my spirits are lifted when I see a clear blue sky and beautiful cloud formations and sunsets.

*　　*　　*

June went on to say:

I now realize that Emily H . . . has written about a cloud experience with one of her Golden Retrievers of the past. I have met Emily nearly every week over more than twenty years and neither of us had breathed a word of what we had seen, to each other or anyone else, until you made it possible.

Sarah

(Emily H's own words – from her letter)

My beloved Golden Retriever, Sarah, passed over at the end of June 1999, aged almost 17 years.

About two weeks after her passing, I was waiting for a local bus, which I rarely use. For no reason, I suddenly looked up and saw, very clearly, in cloud formation, the exact outline of a 'Golden', complete with tail and leg feathers. I stood transfixed. There was no doubt in my mind that it was Sarah. It was almost like watching her in the ring, only in white! I felt she had come to tell me she was not far away.

Jane Lilley

Jane published my request for help in her 'Living With Dogs' column in Dog World. She admits that when she first read my letter she thought it was 'silly' and almost binned it, until she remembered that she had had two ADC experiences of her own! She included them in her column, in validation of my request for help and they are reproduced here with her kind permission.

* * *

'I remember that, in the late 70's, I had a definite ADC with our beloved ruby Cavalier bitch, known affectionately as 'Red Dog', simply because all the Tibetan Spaniels were gold at the time. She always used to travel loose behind the back seat of our estate car.

The day after she was put to sleep, I was backing the car out of the garage and, looking in the mirror, found myself saying 'For goodness sake, get down Red Dog', because, as usual, she was jumping up so I could not see out of the back window. She was quite definitely there.

It was only when I had turned the car round and was driving out of the drive, that I realised that, of course, she was no longer with us but indeed, it was such an incredibly comforting feeling to know that she was very obviously still with us in spirit and, presumably, happy and content wherever she was.

More recently, my late alter ego, Bertha, was constantly at my side whenever I carried a tray of food through from the kitchen to the drawing room. She always did have a gift for slipping unseen through apparently closed doors. This continued, again most comfortingly, for at least a week after she had departed this life. It seemed like a natural progression, call it imagination if you like but her presence was there.'

Anne Roslin-Williams

Like Jane Lilley, Anne is also a regular columnist for Dog World Magazine. The following is reproduced here with her kind permission.

*   *   *

Jane Lilley wrote about some canine revisitations, which put me in mind of the time my mother came to take me out from one of my many boarding schools. As she entered through the front door, the housemistress told her very politely, looking down at my mother's heels, that she was sorry, she could not bring her Labrador in with her, as visitors were not allowed to bring their dogs into the school buildings. Rather surprising to my mother, as she had no dog with her.

Whether that was the shade of a deceased Labrador, or of one left at home, we never knew, but the housemistress had quite clearly seen the black Labrador at my mother's heels.

Ben

(Diane's own words – from her letter)

My Lurcher cross, Ben, aged 8 years, had had a lovely Sunday, walking and swimming in the sea.

That night I had a dream. My mother, who had been dead for 20 years, came to me and said that Ben was ill and that she would take him to the vet, to which I agreed.

After what seemed like hours, (still in my dream), my husband and I went searching for them but to no avail. They had disappeared.

I woke from my sleep in a cold sweat and decided to go downstairs and make a cup of tea. Ben woke up and I said 'Tea Ben'. As he jumped down from the settee his back legs collapsed.

He was at the vet's for four days before he died (and we still miss him) but I do believe that my mother came for him.

Lace

Linda telephoned.

Linda has Golden Retrievers. She remembers well, something that happened approximately seven years ago. Her foundation bitch was Lace; not the most glamorous show-girl, according to Linda, in that she was very big and rather masculine in type but she was extremely loyal, very special to her and they were very close.

Just before her ninth birthday, the vet confirmed that Lace had cancer, something that, sadly, Linda had suspected. Lace was put to sleep just two weeks after the diagnosis was made but according to Linda they made the most of every minute of that time. When the day came to say goodbye, Linda left Lace's body at the vets' to be cremated. She says that she knew that somehow she would come back.

At 3pm the same afternoon, Linda was in the sitting-room with Lace's daughter Silk, who lay staring into the corner where Lace used to lie and then crossed her front legs, something which she had never done before but which Lace used to do all the time. Linda's friend was there at the time and remarked that Lace had come back to say goodbye.

The next day, Linda went to the crematorium to collect Lace's ashes and asked the lady there if she had any idea what time Lace had been cremated. The lady told her that she remembered clearly the clock in the house striking three and Linda just said, 'Yes, I thought so', that being the exact time that Silk had crossed her legs in the way her mother used to.

A couple of days later, Linda was upstairs in the bathroom. She cleaned her teeth and washed her face and in reaching across to get the towel, almost fell over Lace, as she'd instinctively lifted her leg to step over her when she saw her lying there on the bathroom floor. She saw her in entirety for several seconds, just as in life but looking healthy and well, with all her lumps from the cancer gone and her feet, which had been ulcerated from treatment, completely healed.

Some weeks later, Linda and her husband were away on holiday in their caravan. On previous holidays, Lace had always been with them. If Linda's husband needed to get up to go to the loo in the night, he would take the torch and step carefully over the sleeping dogs on the floor. Lace would seize the opportunity to sneak into bed and lie with her back against Linda's back and her legs pushing against the wall of the caravan. So it was no surprise to Linda that on this holiday, when her husband got up to go to the loo, she felt the warmth of Lace behind her back and her pushing against the wall, quite clearly, just as she had in life, until eventually Linda fell asleep. When she woke in the morning, Lace was gone and has not reappeared since.

*　　*　　*

After Lace was diagnosed with cancer (lymphosarcoma), Linda contacted a faith healer, named Sue, in the fervent hope that she might be able to do something to help. Acting with Sue's guidance, Linda tried hands on healing with Lace.

One night, practising this, lying on the floor and drifting off to sleep, Linda was suddenly aware that Lace seemed to have stopped breathing. She watched and listened intently to make sure that Lace was still alive but the breathing got shallower and shallower until she was sleeping so deeply that she was barely moving. Linda never left her for a moment, thinking that at any moment she would be gone. At 5am Lace gave a huge sigh and began breathing normally.

Later that morning, Sue rang. She told Linda that Lace had been to visit her last night, had stayed for several hours and left at 5am. She asked where she got her eyes and what she had done to her tail. Linda says that Lace had slightly protruding eyes, like a Boxer, quite uncharacteristic of a Golden Retriever and because one of Linda's Westies had snapped at Lace's tail and made it bleed, she had put a plastic carton on the end of it, to stop her banging it and making it bleed more.

Linda had only ever spoken to Sue on the phone, so was amazed that she knew about these things because she had never seen Lace. Nothing had ever been mentioned before, that had anything to do with her eyes or tail. Linda knew beyond any doubt that Lace must really have visited Sue the previous night, just as she had said.

*　　*　　*

Linda has a pick of the litter puppy from Jade, another of Lace's daughters. This bitch is very big but has a softer look than Lace had. Linda is convinced that she is Lace reincarnated.

Becky

Frances telephoned.

Becky was Frances's dearly loved Tibetan Spaniel and had all but reached the amazing age of sixteen years when Frances woke one morning in June 2003 to find her dead at her side.

Although Becky had obviously died peacefully in her sleep, it was a shock to Frances and she was naturally very upset.

Some weeks later, returning from the shops, Frances put the key in the front door lock. As she opened the door she heard one welcoming bark from Becky. It sounded so real that she half expected to see her. Frances says, just that one bark gave her a great deal of comfort.

Pip

Ann telephoned.

Ann has had Border Collies for many years but previously she had a pet Sheltie named Pip, who lived to the grand old age of sixteen and a half years. At that time she also had two cats, Susie and Beejay. They all, (along with Ann's husband), lived in a three-storey Victorian house in Chester.

Some while before he died, Pip had a heart attack and went blind. Susie acted as his eyes and would lead him around, especially when they were out in the garden. She in turn, was unable to miaow, due to a fluey-type of illness she'd had and although she had a bell on her collar so that Ann knew where she was; if she wanted anything, Pip would bark for her.

Ann and her husband slept at the top of the house, on the second floor, each floor having a double wooden staircase to the next level. The stairs had a carpet runner in the middle with polished wood either side and the top landing had painted floorboards with a glass panel in the centre. Before his heart attack, Pip would always go upstairs to bed but afterwards he had to stay down as the stairs were just too much for him to manage.

Eventually, inevitably, Pip had to be put to sleep. One night soon after, Ann and her husband were in bed when they heard the sound of nails clacking on the floorboards, first on the stairs and then on the landing. At first, they clung to each other in fright but then, realizing that it was Pip they found it comforting. They only heard it once.

The Cat & Amos

Amy telephoned.

Amy and her friend used to go out to lunch regularly. On one occasion the friend asked if they could go to her mother's house, because her mother wasn't very well. Amy had never been to the house before but had no objections, so off they went.

Two months later, out for lunch again, Amy's friend mentioned that she had just bought a kitten. She also said that she was going away on holiday. Amy asked where she was going to leave the kitten while she was away and her friend said she was leaving it at her mother's. Horrified, Amy said 'You can't do that, that big cat will kill it!' When her friend asked her which cat she meant, Amy said 'The big tabby that was sitting on the arm of the sofa, when we went round for lunch when your mother wasn't well.' Her friend then informed her that he had died three years ago.

Although Amy says she saw the cat quite clearly, she also remembers that she had no desire whatsoever to stroke it, as she would normally have done.

*   *   *

Amy says she has had hundreds of animals in her life but only once has she had one of them come back to 'visit'.

This was a German Shepherd, named Amos, which she took in as a rescue. At first he lived in the house but was always very nervous. Later, after he had been very ill, he became scared of everything, so took to living outside in an old car.

One day, some time after he died, Amy was sitting upstairs on the bed, when a dog literally leapt through the bedroom wall towards her. She recognised it instinctively as Amos and shouted his name. He turned and stared at her for about thirty seconds before he disappeared. Amy says he looked totally bewildered. She was so worried that she prayed to St. Francis, (the Patron Saint of animals) and asked if he would please find him and help him because he seemed so lost.

Six weeks later, Amy's friend told her that she'd had a really strange dream. She said she saw Amos with a man dressed in brown.

Amy believes that her prayer was answered and that this man was St. Francis, who would have been wearing brown because he was a Franciscan monk.

*   *   *

Amy may not actually see any of her other lost friends when they return but she does see a blue light which appears in the dog room at the same time every night.

On the occasions when she has to be away from home, Amy's dogsitters always tell her that her spirit dogs are terribly noisy when she's not there. They are heard continually running up and down the stairs and in and out of the bedroom. The sitters say they are not at all frightened of being alone in the house – they just can't stand the noise!

Holly

Iris telephoned.

Iris is a retired nurse. Her father died from a heart attack in 1974 and shortly afterwards her mother had a stroke, so Iris was nursing her at home. At the time, Iris had a 15 year old Yorkshire Terrier bitch named Holly, who had belonged to her late father, plus two other dogs; a Labrador and a young Yorkie.

When Iris had to go into hospital for surgery, her neighbours kindly offered to look after her mother and Holly, who, because of her age, was to remain at home, whilst the other two dogs went into kennels. Holly had her own small cage, which was always left with its door open, so that she could wander in and out as she wanted.

Iris was due to leave hospital on the Monday night but because she was running a temperature, it was decided to keep her in until the next day. Sadly, Holly died on the Monday night. When she was told, Iris was distraught that she hadn't been with her and asked that Holly's body not be moved until she'd seen her. This done, Holly was then taken to the neighbour's garden and buried under a Magnolia tree.

Iris's mother told her that while she was away, Holly had just sat behind the glass-panelled door, crying all the time. She said she thought Holly had just fretted and pined to death, which was a terrible thing for Iris to hear. Losing Holly was bad enough but the thought that she had pined to death in her absence was even more distressing.

One night, some days later, Iris had a dream. She was in a park and saw her dad walking towards her with Holly in his arms. As he got nearer to her, he said 'Don't worry, she understands. She's OK, she's with me now.' Iris says the dream was so clear and real that she never worried about Holly again afterwards.

* * *

Iris's father used to play the organ. When she moved house the organ went with her. At that time she had a Yorkie named Pandy. Iris remembers one occasion when Pandy was sitting in front of the organ and suddenly started barking; 'going mad' as Iris describes it, yet (as far as Iris could see anyway) there was nothing there.

One Extra(ordinary) Dog

Sarah wrote to say:

It's a relief to know that I am not the only one to have a beloved dog return and take up residence again!

I lost my little man two years ago at the age of 12 years. He had survived two accidents, one very serious, and prostate cancer. He finally succumbed to kidney failure. He lived nine months longer than was expected; so he obviously had a strong will to live.

Within days (of his passing) I was seeing him about the house out of the corner of my eye; out in the garden with the other (four) dogs, pottering about on our walks. Time and again I have counted four dogs into the house, shut the door, heard a bark and found one dog still outside.

The strongest sighting came last year. I was attacked by a vicious bug and had to take to my bed. For two weeks I was extremely ill, staggering out of bed only to go to the loo or to get a drink. My friend came and took my four dogs away to look after them so that I did not have the worry of them. Almost at once, my boy appeared and sat on the bed with me through all those days of my illness. When I woke from sleep I could feel the weight of him against my legs and the warmth coming through the duvet. When I rose to make tea I would come back and find the area of the bed where I had been lying still warm. He stayed very visible until the other dogs came back and then seemed to feel I could cope again. He is still around but content now to stay at the edge of my vision.

I know people will explain these things by saying 'wishful thinking' or 'imagination' but I know it is more than that. I have kept dogs for many years and all have been special and beloved but he is the only one to have come back. I lost my husband just six weeks after my boy and I sometimes wonder if this is why he has returned.

Incidentally, my husband has never returned, although one of my other dogs saw something for weeks after his death and would not walk round the side of my sofa and also whined and scraped at the front door, wagging her tail. I found this unnerving and a little scary but have never worried about my little man's presence.

Larry

(Sheila's own words – from her note)

We had our first, pet Sheltie, nearly 40 years ago. He was large for a Sheltie and we called him Larry. When he developed a cyst on his back, our local vet insisted on a major operation. Larry died under anaesthetic. He was just 7 years old.

My husband worked shifts at the time and when I was alone, especially in the evenings when the children were in bed, I could 'feel' Larry by my side wherever I went.

Five months after his death, we bought a puppy. As soon as she entered the house I felt a little sigh and I never felt Larry again. It was as though he said "You'll be OK now mum."

Friday

(From Rachel's letter)

Rachel has always owned and loved Elkhounds and Siamese cats. She says that of all the animals she has had, only one has ever appeared to her and she has never forgotten the experience. This was her very first Siamese, a female, named 'Friday'.

One afternoon, a week after Friday's death, Rachel was upstairs in the bedroom, when 'Friday' appeared at the side of the bed. She walked very slowly across the room and disappeared into the wardrobe – which was closed!

Rachel says that following this, the calmness she felt was wonderful. When her husband appeared he knew immediately that something had happened and when Rachel told him, he didn't for one instant question it, as he usually would.

For many years, Rachel wondered why Friday was the only one, out of all her wonderful pets, to ever come back to see her. Her conclusion is this. Friday was nine years old and had been at the vet's for five days. The vet guaranteed that he would get her well enough to return home but sadly this was not to be. Friday died unexpectedly whilst she was still at the surgery.

She was the only one of Rachel's animals that has ever died away from home. All the others have been put to sleep by the vet, at home. Rachel was distraught because she hadn't been with Friday when she died. She believes that this was Friday's way of letting her know that all was now well and that she'd come to see her for the final time. Following 'Friday's' visit, Rachel says she was able to 'go about her business with no recriminations.'

Tyn

Ros runs a rescue kennels. She currently has 49 permanent residents, the oldest of which is 19 years. She never re-homes any animal that comes into her care as a rescue but lets them live out their lives happily with their contemporaries. As many of them are well into their teens, she obviously has the right formula!

A while ago she lost a 15 year old sheepdog bitch named Scruffy, who always liked to lie on hay, hidden behind bales, out of the way of people and other dogs. The morning Scruffy died, Ros told the kennel girls to leave Scruffys body where it was for the time being, hidden as usual behind bales inside the barn.

Ros says that one of the other elderly dogs Tyn, who couldn't see the body from where he was and who, Ros believes, was unlikely to pick up her scent, started pointing towards where she lay; at the same time growling and barking madly. Her body was moved later that same day.

The following morning Tyn again went quite berserk as he reached the same spot where he barked from the previous day.

The next morning exactly the same thing happened. Tyn growled and barked continuously until they took him to the spot where Scruffy had died and told him everything was OK. He now passes that place without any problems.

Bramble & Oscar

Jenny wrote.

My sister is the Secretary/Treasurer of Labrador Welfare and we were upset to hear from one of our foster homes, that Bramble, one of our older dogs, had been diagnosed with an inoperable cancer on his face.

A few days later, his former owner rang to ask how he was. She was upset and said that she had felt something was wrong because she had been out in her car a few days previously, when she had smelt Bramble in the back. She had thought this odd, as she had not smelt him in the car since he had been rehomed.

Another incident involved one of her own dogs.

Jenny wrote:

Shortly before she died, my mother told me that she had dreamt that horrible things were being done to Oscar, our chocolate Labrador. At the time I just thought it was an elderly lady having bad dreams. However, when Oscar was diagnosed with osteosarcoma last year, her words came back to me. Horrible things really did happen to him.

When he was alive, I could sometimes smell the sweet smell that so often seems to be around cancer patients. I could still smell this on occasions after his death, until one night I had a very vivid dream.

In the dream, I looked down to see Oscar walking up behind me. He had no swelling on his shoulder and his face was bright and full of mischief, as it always had been. Perhaps people will say that this was because I wanted to believe that he was out of pain but either way it has given me comfort, although we still miss him so much.

and

One other thing. For a month after our budgie died, I used to hear him swinging on his perch – and we had given the cage away!

Daisy

Kay wrote.

We lost our dear Westie, Daisy, a few years ago. She had a very swollen stomach, so I made an appointment with the vet and my husband took her in. Before she went, I said, 'Don't worry Daisy, mummy will pick you up.' The vet phoned to say that she had cirrhosis of the liver and there was no hope for her. She was just five years old.

We had bought her from a kennels in Dartmouth. The puppies had been put on a train in Scotland and sold in Devon. She was a wonderful dog and the whole family was heartbroken. We had another dog, Jock, at the time (who lived till he was fifteen) and one day, about three weeks after Daisy died, I was feeding Jock his supper, when I looked down and there was Daisy. No imagination, she was there. It lasted for about six seconds.

I rushed into the kitchen and told my husband that I'd just seen Daisy. 'Never' he said, 'You must have been seeing things.' I was adamant. 'Fine' I said, 'I know what I saw.'

A week later, my husband was out in the garden at dusk. It was a warm summer night. Daisy always loved the garden at that time of night and would sit outside, trying to catch flies. Suddenly, my husband came rushing indoors. 'Kay' he said, 'I've just seen Daisy snapping flies!'

None of us have ever seen her again. We wonder if she came back to say goodbye?

Chelidh

Pam has Bernese Mountain Dogs and Polish Lowland Sheepdogs. Her first Bernese was a bitch named Chelidh; a name chosen for her, because Pam says, 'She was like a Highland fling.' Chelidh was extremely devoted to Pam and her husband and when they walked the dogs on the beach, although the others would all run about and play, Chelidh would stay close by Pam's legs, content to watch but all the time knowing exactly where the others were.

At just 5years of age, Chelidh died of cancer. For a long time afterwards, Pam says they could still feel her presence alongside them whenever they walked on the beach and always had the impression that Chelidh was watching the others as she always used to.

Bess

Phyllis wrote:

I have always had Flatcoat Retrievers. My first two were sisters, Bess and Emma. Bess had to be put to sleep when she was eight years old.

A few months after, when taking Emma out, we were walking in a field with no-one else around. Emma was well ahead in front of me, when I became conscious of another dog walking by my side. This dog had on a blue collar, which Bess always wore.

I looked around for Emma, who was still out in front. When I looked again at my side, Bess had gone. I know it was her from the way she always looked up at me.

It was such a strange feeling that I thought I must have imagined it but it was so real, I know it was her. It was such a lovely feeling to think she came back, even if only for a short time. I have never seen her since.

Xerxes

(Rosemary's own words – from her letter)

Xerxes was an outstanding Saluki who gained his championship in the show ring (gaining one CC out of veteran!). However, it was on the coursing field that he really excelled. In his coursing years, he won most of the available trophies and could always be relied upon to run a good course.

He died from old age on a Friday in the midst of the coursing season.

The following day, his owner and the rest of us were out coursing, when we noticed one cloud in an otherwise clear sky. The shape of Xerxes was quite clear in the cloud, which hovered over the slipper for some time.

One of Xerxes' 'relatives' was in slips and as soon as the hounds were slipped the cloud vanished rapidly. We all felt that Xerxes had gone to follow the course!

Bunty & Dexter

Jean and her husband Mark have had two occasions when their departed dogs have returned to them.

Jean wrote:

When we lived in Walthamstow, E.17, our dear Corgi, called Bunty, had died. Some months later we were looking out of the kitchen window, when we both said, 'Look, there's Bunty!' He was trotting about in the garden and then he just vanished.

* * *

After Bunty died we had a Beagle called Dexter. One evening, on our usual walk in Epping Forest, we heard him give one cry but he had vanished. We couldn't find him anywhere, even though we searched and called for hours. We were absolutely frantic. For a week we had friends searching, the Police were informed but still no Dexter.

Then one night, still searching the same area where we had last seen him, looking across the road, I saw Dexter sitting there, near a street light, number 138. We raced across the road but there was nothing there. The next morning we went back. There, lying in the bushes, was Dexter's body. It had obviously been there a week. We can only guess that he must have died instantly of a heart attack. The Police were very kind and agreed that we could bury him in the forest, which as we didn't have a car could otherwise have been a worry.

We were grateful at least, to know his end and not to have to worry over the years, what had happened to him; dreading the thought that he might have been stolen for experiments.

* * *

Our daughter Mary, lives in Wickford. She often feels the presence of their Afghan, Tara, who died years ago. Some weeks ago, their cat Fluffy, came up onto the bed and made a real fuss of them, purring all the time. Within ten minutes she died. It was as if she had been saying goodbye.

Crystal

Celia wrote to me on some very pretty notepaper with a huge Red Admiral butterfly in the bottom right-hand corner. In my reply, I asked if she knew that butterflies were spirit signs. Just as I wrote the question a Red Admiral appeared outside the barn window where I was working. When she replied, she said that, no, she had no idea.

*   *   *

Celia wrote:

I lost my dearly loved young Sheltie, Crystal, in May this year, through a tragic road accident. Later the same evening, after a harrowing time, I was in the bath, trying to relax, when suddenly I was aware of Crystal being there. She often used to look in on me in the bathroom. As I was more aware, she was gone. I remember thinking to myself 'Oh, you've come to say goodbye.'

I'm certain my other Shelties were all downstairs. It may have been wishful thinking on my part but I did feel a link and some comfort.

Bridgette

Brenda wrote to me about her experience following the death of her beloved American Cocker bitch, Bridgette, who she lost to cancer, aged 13 years. At the time, Brenda had two Cockers, the other being Bridgette's devoted companion, Shane. When Bridgette died, Brenda and Shane both missed her dreadfully but her photograph and ashes were kept on the kitchen shelf and Brenda says this was a comfort.

*   *   *

Brenda wrote:

One morning, almost two years after Bridgette's death, feeling rather depressed about a new home I was purchasing, I sat in front of the patio doors with my coffee, when suddenly, I saw 'my girl' appear amidst the clouds. She looked happy, almost smiling but appeared to have wings and unicorn horn. I quickly sketched her in disbelief, as I'm not a believer in life after death or ghosts, or at least I wasn't, should I say!

I cried as she slowly disappeared but felt some contentment also. Now, on cloudy days, I constantly scan the skies for a glimpse of her and her companion 'Shane', who I lost recently aged 11 years. His ashes and photograph sit alongside Bridgette's, together in life and now, hopefully together, pain free, my 'babies' are running or flying round the Heavens, chasing their tennis ball.

A Wealth Of Experiences

Sara wrote.

When I was a child there was a white Jack Russell type terrier that used to appear from time to time on our farm. My mother saw it several times just after we moved to the farm and fearing that it might be lost, reported it to the local Post Office. After meaningful glances were exchanged, it was explained to her that it was a ghost dog, probably owned by a previous incumbent of the house, which was over 400 years old and that many people had seen it.

My first encounter with it was when I was about seven. Returning home from school one day, it suddenly ran past me as I walked up the path to our front door. As I opened the door it simply vanished. During the years we lived at the farm, we all saw it from time to time, although I never saw it as closely as on that first occasion. Usually it was pottering about in our front field, just as any dog would do.

*   *   *

When I was about eighteen, my parents had a house whose central heating was powered by an ancient solid fuel boiler, which was housed in a sort of outside cellar with a roof over it. One evening I offered to fill the boiler as my mother wasn't well. As I struggled down the steps to it, carrying a full hod of coal, I found her Alsatian (as they were called then) bitch, lying across the top of the steps. This was typical as she always managed to stretch out in doorways etc. 'Oh Bracken, do get out of the way', I moaned as I stepped over her. Having filled the boiler, I glanced up and saw Bracken still watching me with interest – then she disappeared! With a jolt I remembered that we had had her put to sleep three days earlier. It certainly wasn't a case of expecting her to be there because I lived away from home and I think it was the first time I'd ever filled the boiler.

*   *   *

We had Alsatians for many years. After our last one, Kuhayla, died in 1987, aged 13, I was walking across the car park at our nursery, when I suddenly saw her, sitting up and watching me, from about 50 feet away. I called my husband but sadly she faded away from sight before he left the potting shed.

*   *   *

I had a very much-loved pony for 20 years. He sadly passed on, aged 30, in 2000 and is now buried in our paddock. Although I haven't actually seen him, several times I've felt his presence very strongly and in my mind I have seen a very vivid picture of him standing, ears pricked, looking very intently at me. At the same time I've had a strong feeling that he has come back to see if I am OK and to tell me how well he is.

*   *   *

In the early 1990's, one of our Whippets became terribly ill. The vets tried every sort of test but everything came back normal, despite the fact that the dog had a temperature of 105–106 degrees F, wouldn't/ couldn't eat or drink, had a very irregular heartbeat and was clearly fading fast. No antibiotics or pills had any effect and in the end I desperately sent out prayers for his recovery. Though not a Churchgoer, I have a strong belief in the Almighty and Jesus Christ and believe in the powers of prayer.

One night, distraught about our little dog, I begged for some help and to know whether we should actually put him out of his misery. As I sat there, I suddenly 'saw' an extraordinary scene. Our two Whippets were romping and playing gleefully in our field, amidst long green grass and under a clear blue sky. In my picture, I was standing beside our house looking across a blue and gold flowerbed into the paddock. At the same time, I experienced an intense feeling of calm and the certainty that the dog would be alright.

It all lasted a few seconds and as the picture faded, I realized with a shock, that what I had been looking at was a scene for the following summer, as it was now November. The blue and gold flowerbed had only just been planted and was presently nothing more than bare earth with a few twigs visible.

Sure enough, our dog shortly began to recover and went on to become perfectly healthy again, living for another six years or so. The following summer I did indeed stand by the house, looking over the blue and gold bed in all its glory and gave immense thanks as I watched our two dogs playing happily in the long grass of the paddock, under a clear blue sky.

* * *

I had a similar experience with the pony I mentioned earlier. He and I had an extraordinary rapport during the 20 years that I owned him, more so than any of the hundreds of horses and ponies I've owned over nearly 60 years.

Eventually he had to be put down because the vets diagnosed a brain tumour. Naturally, I was deeply upset about this and very emotional. I was fortunate in that I was able to have him put down at home and he is buried in our field in the place he used to love to stand by.

The evening after this had taken place, I felt not only drained but guilty about whether I could have made his last few days better or more comfortable. Once again, I sat and prayed for some help. Suddenly, there was a sort of 'wide screen' in front of me and I was looking at a glorious picture of rolling grassland, dotted with heads of horses. The colours were beyond anything I've ever seen on this earth. Then, just like a movie, a herd of horses and ponies galloped across the 'screen' from right to left. They were wild and joyous, manes and tails flying, tossing their heads and moving so effortlessly.

In the middle of them was my pony, a very distinctive roan, surrounded by all manner of horses of all colours. I thought I recognised two ponies I had known in the past also there. As the herd thundered silently by, at the very rear was a small dark brown Dartmoor pony, bucking and kicking for joy. There was no doubt that it was a Dartmoor that I had owned until his death, aged 27 and who, for eleven years, was the devoted companion of Sherbet, the roan.

Once again, this fabulous scene only lasted seconds but the pure happiness and joy of those horses filled me and almost made me cry with pleasure. It was so beautiful. Once again also, I felt unbelievable calm and thrill that Sherbet was now with his 'people' and young and free and happy. It was a complete miracle, which even now fills me with emotion.

*   *   *

It would appear that Sara's animals were able to see their contemporaries too, as she also wrote:

Many years ago we had a strange corner of a paddock, which all our horses avoided like the plague. It looked to us to be perfectly normal, no overhanging trees, nothing dark or spooky. In fact, it was where two paddocks met, with an open track between them. Whenever we put a new horse in that field, if it was grazing quietly across the paddock, as soon as it got within 30–50 yards of that corner, its head would go up, there would be a snort and off it would gallop. This happened even if no other horses were in the field.

I've also seen about four of our ponies careering round as they do but as soon as they got near 'the corner', the leader would wheel away and hi-tail it to a safer distance.

We often wondered if a carthorse had been buried there and whether the ponies could see a 'ghost' horse.

Ray Gildea

Ray is a medium and has had many ADC experiences. He has written a leaflet entitled 'Pets on the Other Side of Life', which details some of his experiences with animals in the spirit world. With his kind permission it is reproduced in part here.

I had heard many mediums pass on information on pets – from cats, dogs and budgies to exotic creatures such as snakes and parrots – but it was not until March 1995, when our cat Fluffy died, that I was privileged to make contact with spirit animals.

We had taken her to the vet to be put to sleep and my mother-in-law, May who was regularly in contact with me from the Spirit World, told me she had taken Fluffy over and she went in with her tail high.

A few days later, May and Fluffy appeared in front of me and I was dumbfounded when Fluffy looked at me and said – yes said! – in a soft feminine voice 'Try and stop me getting up now!' I had always tried to deter her from jumping on to my wife's knee and padding on her legs, plucking her clothes. Having said that, Fluffy just jumped on to my wife's knee and started padding about.

I must admit that the thought of an animal speaking in a human voice was disconcerting and I was quite upset by it. People have enough trouble believing that family and friends who have passed over can actually speak to you, without trying to convey an animal's words!

Apparently, animals can only reincarnate as animals, whereas a human can take on an animal life-form for earthly experiences but can later reincarnate as a human. I have been led to believe that Fluffy was a human who had come to earth to try life as a cat.

From the first time Fluffy appeared to me, she has often appeared in our home and garden but has only spoken to me occasionally. Usually, as all cats do, she stretches out in front of the fire or under the shade of a tree, depending where she is.

Although my wife cannot see Spirit, she knows when Fluffy is in our living room as the leaves on the plant at ground level move as she brushes against them. My wife has also seen the curtains move and I was able to tell her it was Fluffy chasing a fly.

Also in 1995, my sister-in-law's pet dog, Basil, passed away. May brought him along one night, saying he was well and with her.

On another occasion, soon after a headstone had been erected on his grave in my sister-in-law's garden, Basil spoke to me in a normal man's voice. 'Thanks for the headstone. I'm glad she's got a bitch (Meg) because she can't cock her leg up on it. Tell Mrs. Sylvia thanks for taking me in. I could never show my gratitude but I will never forget her'. (Sylvia had taken Basil in as a stray and, following his death, had obtained a bitch as a pet.)

On more than one occasion, when Sylvia and my wife have been talking together, Basil has appeared alongside Sylvia and Fluffy alongside my wife but Fluffy is always wary of Basil and keeps an eye on him.

When Meg (Sylvia's bitch) passed away, I saw a lovely picture of Basil trotting alongside her, leading her to the Other Side, where May met them and patted Meg's head. May has told me she often takes Basil for a walk but Meg has decided to reincarnate and Sylvia has been told to watch out for an unusually coloured squirrel!

At the end of November 1999, I was surprised when Fluffy came through and said she had been working around an earthquake site, leading dogs to the victims who were trapped. (This indicated that animals work on the Other Side, just like people who have passed over.) She lay on her side in front of the fire saying 'My paws are cut to ribbons but I won't get any blood on the carpet'. I felt she had come home to rest.

Merry & The Springers

Laura has been fortunate, since childhood, to have contact with many of her animals that have passed After writing to me in the first instance, there followed a long telephone conversation in which she provided me with a great deal of background information, included here.

*   *   *

Laura used to have pre-cognitive dreams, usually of disasters, always disturbing, until eventually she was referred to a child psychiatrist, who told her parents to 'Get her to write about her dreams – or draw pictures.' One dream that she remembers particularly well, was about three trains that crashed. The crash happened just days later.

All Laura ever wanted was to be with animals. She persuaded her parents to let her work at a local kennels. Although she was only eleven or twelve years old at the time, she went, on her own, to the kennels and asked if she could work there. They took her on with no payment but training in lieu, as many places did in those days, according to Laura who is in her 60's now. Apparently, rich people kennelled their dogs and only took them home when they wanted to show them off.

When she left these kennels two years later, Laura was asked if she would like one of the dogs to keep as her own. There were two that she particularly liked but eventually she chose a poodle dog named Merry and he went home to live with her and her family.

Some time later they were all going away on holiday. Much to Laura's dismay, her parents said that Merry had to go back to stay at the kennels. Four days into the holiday they met up with one of the kennel-maids who told them that Merry was ill.

After a great deal of persuasion, Laura's parents finally agreed to take her back to see him but she had to wait until the next day. When they eventually arrived at the kennels, the owners refused to let her see Merry, saying that he had a brain tumour. Laura was distraught and he died without her ever seeing him again. The night he died, she had a dream in which Merry was leaping about and running round, healthy and happy. She called her mother and said 'Mum, Merry's here.' Sadly, her mother thought that she was having dreams again, like she used to and said she would have to go back to the doctor's.

* * *

Another of Laura's childhood pets was a big ginger cat called Monty, who she used to dress up and wheel to the village and back in a pram. He would follow her to school and meet her when she came out and although at home he was not allowed upstairs he always managed to sneak up and join her in bed. He was old by the time she got married and had to stay behind at her parent's house because she was in the services.

Laura was upset that he died while she was away but shocked when, getting off the bus to visit her parents one day, she saw Monty on the corner of the street. He ran down the road, looking over his shoulder as he always did and into her parents' house. Laura says she got some weird looks when she said, 'I thought you said Monty had died?' No ginger cats had been seen in the area before, nor were for a long time afterwards.

* * *

Despite the fact that she grew up in a household that didn't accept her experiences as anything more than childish imagination, Laura was always convinced that what was happening was very special. She found and still finds it very comforting. She believes that perhaps our lost pets come back to comfort us when we are upset and to let us know that they are alright. Hopefully now, we're moving into more enlightened times.

* * *

(Laura's own words – from her letter)

I lost Sam, one of my English Springer Spaniels, at five and a half years of age. All the dogs were special to me in their way but, like some people, Sam had that little bit extra about him. When he was put to sleep I was devastated and the next day, walking the other dogs across the fields, I felt choked and just could not stop the tears running down my face. In fact, as the weeks went by, I wondered if there would ever come a day when I did not feel totally lost without him, or my eyes remain dry.

It was a still autumn morning, with quite a heavy early frost. I remember stopping and shuddering, as I tried to take a deep breath and relieve the ache in my throat as I looked out across the grasses. It was the far away barking that made me listen up, as immediately I thought 'Sam'. Just as always, there in the distance was Sam, running through the grasses, round and round, barking with delight and every now and then jumping up to see where I was. Like a fool I called out his name, moving forward at the same time towards him, thinking, 'He's not dead' (although I was with him to the end, at the vet's); that somehow he must have come round and got out.

My other dogs, who would normally have been doing the same as Sam but without the barking, had been sitting quietly at my feet but they had shot up and dashed off in the same direction. Then the grasses became still again, apart from the waves the others were making and Sam's voice faded away. The dogs stopped in their tracks – looking – and then came back.

Nine times out of ten we had this early morning walk to ourselves, just like that morning, when my Springers were the only ones in the area. Writing this, I feel the whole experience again, as fresh as if it was today, tears as well. No one will ever convince me that it was only an illusion, as for a very long time I felt his presence over there and seeing him so happy did help me accept my loss.

She continued:

As Poppy, (also an E.S.S.), was getting old, she was going deaf. I bought a babies small musical house which played a tune when you pulled a string and hung it on the side of the kitchen cabinet. Poppy would sit in the doorway between the kitchen and the hallway and wait for me to pull the string so she could listen to it. I don't know whether she could hear the tinkling sound, or whether she just watched the movement but she obviously liked it. For a long time after Poppy died, I would see her in my mind's eye and feel her pressing against the back of my legs as I stood near the worktop in the kitchen. It would be so real that I would lift my leg to step over her when I turned round. Exactly the same thing would happen when I was sitting in my chair. I would feel Poppy's weight lying across my feet.

*   *   *

George was the last of Laura's dogs.

She wrote:

George, also an English Springer Spaniel, became incontinent (rear end) for the last eighteen months of his life. Most times he would make it to the garden but sometimes he would do it in his sleep. Sitting not far away, I would think – that's definitely not wind and would remove it without him even waking up. Somewhile after he passed; engrossed partly in watching TV and partly in reading a book, I suddenly thought, 'Oh dear, George has had an accident', grabbed some tissues and got up to go to his bed which would have been to the side of me – and then stopped dead in my tracks.

Silly me. No George. This has happened several times and I'm certain it's his way of letting me know it's him and that he's here with me. At these times I do acknowledge him, just as I did to Sam when his presence was felt when walking over the field. If I'm honest, I don't ever want that contact to be severed. I would like to continue to believe that there is more to life after this one. The up side of moments like this is that feeling of the place coming to life again. The down side, the cold emptiness when back to reality but I still feel much happier for the contacts.

The night before George was taken, he had a short walk up the road but unlike him, he was being stubborn and would not turn back, facing in the direction of the field.

He couldn't manage to walk both ways as well as round the field and he was too heavy for me to carry any distance if his legs gave out, so eventually I did manage to persuade him to come back. As I didn't have a car, I acquired a child buggy some time ago, actually for Lucy (another E.S.S.) before she died but now using it for George so that he could enjoy longer outings, walking one way and riding back.

I put George in the buggy and off we went to the field. I was sitting on the bench with George beside me, when he got up and stared hard into the field. He wasn't a barker but he gave several small woofs, looked at me and wagged his tail, then stared hard again. For a second, I felt and almost expected to see, the others come running towards us but the field was quiet and empty. I patted him and said 'Yes George, sometimes mummy thinks she can see them playing as well.' I took him home with a terrible, though long expected, sinking feeling inside.

I stayed with him as he slowly faded that night. He died quietly in my arms the next morning. I would love to think that my other lovely, dearly missed companions had come for him to go and play, in what I think was one of their favourite walk and swimming areas, close to our home.

Jet

Tracey has had three separate and all quite different ADC experiences to date.

*   *   *

At one time, she worked at a Great Dane kennels where she lived-in. One of the 'oldies', a black dog named Jet, (about 10 or 11 years of age), had, in Tracey's words, 'been very poorly' and so, was allowed to sleep in the bedroom of her boss, Hilda. One morning, Tracey got up for work as usual, around 7.30am. She walked along the landing to the bathroom and, passing Jet at the top of the stairs as she often did, she said good morning to him and carried on with her normal routine, getting ready for work.

As she sat down for breakfast a while later, Hilda's husband told her that Jet had died during the night, at 4.30am.

Tracey looked at him in disbelief and said 'He can't have. I passed him on the landing at half-past seven this morning and said good morning to him!'

Nothing would convince her that Jet had died until she was taken to see his body, which was still lying at the foot of the bed in Hilda's bedroom.

*   *   *

One of Tracey's own dogs was a Pointer called Sabre. He was bought as a two year old and she had him for ten years. When he was about nine he had a stroke and as a result, over the following three years, his health gradually deteriorated. Tracey was working full-time then but always went home at lunchtime to see to her dogs, letting them out into the garden first of all. Sabre would go to the loo and then come back to the door, jumping up and down and making funny noises until he was let in again.

After he died, Tracey heard the same noise every day for about three weeks.

*   *   *

'Crisp' was a brindle Gt. Dane dog, bred by Tracey and sold as a puppy at 8–9 weeks old. Although she didn't see him after he left her, she kept in contact with Crisp's new owners throughout his life. Despite this, when he was about five and a half years old and became ill with heart problems, they didn't tell her.

Completely unbeknown to Tracey, their vet was having trouble regulating Crisp's heartbeat, so he was sent to Bristol Veterinary Hospital. On the Sunday afternoon, Bristol rang the owners to say that he was doing well and they could collect him on the Monday.

Tracey was eating tea on that particular Sunday, when she suddenly thought of Crisp and had the overwhelming feeling that something had happened to him. Twenty minutes later the phone rang. It was Crisp's owners, to say they had just received a phone call from Bristol telling them that Crisp had died unexpectedly.

Fin

Lily wrote to me to say that she had owned many animals in her 82 years but she believes that there is always 'that special one'.

*   *   *

To her, this was a Swedish Vallhund that she bred and kept, named Fin. Lily describes him as 'rather a dominant little chap, with both endearing and aggravating ways.' She says that he was very special to her and they were very close Three years ago, at the age of ten and a half, Fin became very ill and had to be put to sleep. Lily was devastated.

Occasionally now, she has the feeling that he is still around because she hears him bark and has to stop and think to herself 'What is he barking for?'

Brea

Tessa sent me an e-mail to tell me about a dream she'd had after she lost her Great Dane, Brea, with cancer.

* * *

She wrote:

Brea was diagnosed with Osteosarcoma in her rear right leg, in August 2002. My husband and I weren't sure what course of action to take. The tumour seemed to grow overnight, so we opted for amputation without any chemotherapy. She lived for nine months after she was first diagnosed.

She had some trouble with weakness in her remaining rear leg and the foot was always becoming worn, so she always had some discomfort throughout the nine months.

In February 2003, I took her into the vets', as she seemed to be breathing rather heavily. They found a spot on her lungs. By April she wasn't sleeping at all, so I took her back to the vets. They found a tumour wrapped around her trachea. We were told to take her home and love her.

On May 12th, we had to make the final decision. By this time she had stopped even coming to bed at night, she would just lie in her chair, looking sad and uncomfortable. Throughout the entire illness, she had been on medication to help her breathing and to relieve the pain but her lifestyle had changed drastically. There were no more walks and very few rides as she couldn't jump into the car, but we adapted and changed as well. We made up new games. I made homemade treats and started feeding her a homemade diet. Although I know she missed her old life, she seemed happy with her new one. We had always been 'joined at the hip' and when she was ill I stayed with her as much as possible.

After Brea was put to sleep I had a dream. I dreamt that a friend (that I met on the Canine Bone Cancer message board), lived down the street from me and I dropped Brea off with her while I went for a visit with my Grandmother. Brea had all four legs and no cancer. My friend had two dogs, (one of which is still alive and just diagnosed as Cancer free, after having an amputation and chemotherapy two years ago; the other died a few years ago).

When I returned from visiting my Grandmother, my friend was walking all three dogs on leashes. None of them had missing limbs and all were cancer free. We all played with the dogs and other members of the CBC group were there too. It was as if we were all friends but not because we had been brought together through our cancer dogs. My friend and her husband who were watching Brea, had 3 year old twin boys in the dream, though in real life they don't have children and she is 50 years old.

So I guess I figured that, since this girl and I are such good friends, that Brea and her dog that died, have teamed up and were trying to show me that they are happy and healthy again and living the life that they were once used to.

Not a very exciting dream – but I've felt so much better since having it. I think that, since Brea and I were so close, that she knew that she somehow had to get to me to let me know how she was doing – that she was all better, just like I told her, that when she left me, she would be in a happy place with other dogs and the cancer wouldn't hurt her anymore.

The following three experiencers all know each other through their breed, Great Danes. They had spoken to each other (but no-one else except those directly involved), about their experiences, before my first letter appeared in *Our Dogs*.

*   *   *

Lacey

Joanne only very recently lost her much-loved veteran Great Dane bitch, Lacey. (It wasn't that long ago that I recall seeing Lacey win a huge veteran bitch class at a Breed Show – and how wonderful she looked. I remember the tears of pure joy that Joanne cried and how bursting with pride she was; quite deservedly so.)

Although she has a beautiful young bitch growing nicely and waiting in the wings to follow in Lacey's footsteps, to Joanne, the loss of her old favourite was a devastating blow.

*   *   *

Joanne says that, as Lacey got older, her muzzle used to smell 'like dirty old socks'. Some time after she died, Joanne was in the kitchen cooking dinner. She turned round with a saucepan in her hand and briefly caught the familiar smell of Lacey's muzzle. This has happened again since but the smell has been stronger. On each occasion, she has acknowledged Lacey by saying 'Mummy loves you', as she always did.

Joanne says that after each occurrence, she has felt very calm and reassured, even though at other times she is still finding it hard to cope with her grief.

Elijah

Jill has had dogs for many years, Great Danes being her favourite breed.

On 24ᵗʰ February 2003, her Gt. Dane, Elijah, was put to sleep at the age of eight and a half years. She says that although he had an eye removed when he was just four years old, he always had a great sense of humour and his party piece was to stick his nose up her bum when she was in the shower. (Only a Gt. Dane could get away with that!).

Although Jill has other dogs, Elijah was her heart dog and she missed him deeply when he was gone. She says that when he was alive, he used to make a very strange noise, peculiar to him, like a combination of a playful throat grumble and that slobbery jowel-shaking slapping noise that Danes make. None of her other dogs do it.

One day, after Elijah had been put to sleep, she was in the kitchen making toast, when she heard that very noise right behind her. She turned round and although there was a dog in the kitchen, Jill is certain the noise didn't come from there.

Some days later, she was in the garden, picking up after the dogs, when she felt a nose poke her up the bum. She thought it was one of the dogs but when she turned around, there were no dogs about. She felt that it must be Elijah but didn't say anything to anyone.

Two or three weeks later, Jill's friend Ivy, Ivy's daughter Brenda and Brenda's husband, were visiting her and they all sat indoors having a cup of tea. Brenda wandered out into the garden with her tea and when she came back, she said she'd been poked in the bum, twice, at which point Jill told them about Elijah's visits.

The same thing happened on several occasions, until eventually Jill was getting upset because she felt that Elijah was staying out of loyalty to her. So, one day she went into the garden and told Elijah that she loved him but that it was time for him to go and find the others now. Since when, his visits have stopped.

*   *   *

After Brenda's confirmation of events, Jill contacted a medium, who re-united her with many of her old dogs. One of these was a rescue

Greyhound called Seamus. He had been terminally ill when Jill took him in and sadly she only had him for ten months before he died. The medium told her that he must have been extremely happy in his life with her, to come through as he did. Her mother and father also came through, surrounded by her old dogs.

* * *

This is Brenda's version of events at Jill's house, on the afternoon of one of Elijah's visits:

* * *

'I was with my husband and my mother at Jill's house. We were all enjoying a cup of tea in the lounge but it was a lovely sunny day and I thought it was a shame to waste it by sitting indoors, so I wandered outside, taking my tea with me. When I was just a few feet away from the patio doors, I felt something poke me in the bum. I looked round quickly, expecting to see one of Jill's dogs but none were about. Thinking I must have imagined it, I moved a few steps – the same thing happened again. This time it was a real poke, no mistake but still no sign of a dog, or anything else'

'When I went back indoors, I was reluctant to say anything at first, in case the others laughed at me. The conversation was about dogs (as usual) and eventually I said I was sure something had poked me in the bum while I had been outside. I felt silly as soon as I'd said it, because I thought the others might think I was just trying to 'steal the limelight', until Jill said that exactly the same thing had happened to her on several occasions and she was certain it was Elijah as that was his favourite trick when he was alive! '

* * *

Brenda recalls another experience she had about four of five years ago:

*   *   *

Brenda works part-time as a cleaner. The lady she works for used to have an elderly dog called Kim, who had a metal name disc attached to her collar, which used to jingle as she moved about.

Eventually, through old age, Kim had to be put to sleep. For three or four weeks afterwards, Brenda would still hear Kim's name disc jingling while she was at work. Kim's owner said she heard it too.

Brenda thinks the strangest part about this is that Kim was put to sleep at the vets'. Obviously her spirit had returned home!

Laddie

Margaret wrote to me.

She says in her letter that soon after their marriage, she and her husband acquired a small working sheepdog named Laddie. He was five years old and was advertised in a local paper 'Free to a good home', as his owners were emigrating to New Zealand.

According to Margaret, he was always rather naughty. He was something of an escape artist and would sneak upstairs to lie on the bed when he thought they wouldn't notice. When they called to him, they would hear a thump as he jumped down from the bed and landed on the floor.

He died in 1978, at the ripe old age of seventeen and a half years and Margaret says that, several times after his death, over the course of several weeks, she would be sitting downstairs and hear a thump, just as though Laddie was jumping off the bed. She says that at the time she thought it 'A little eerie'.

Moss, Rusty & Sparky

Hilary e-mailed to say that she has had visits from three of her dogs that have passed.

*   *   *

I am 59 and have owned dogs and cats all my life. My main breed was Pembroke Corgis but I have also owned a Wire Fox Terrier, Cocker Spaniels, a Border Collie and cats. Since 1968, my breed has been Shetland Sheepdogs (Shelties).

One day I was feeding my Shelties. They tend to be very noisy at feeding time, so I called to my husband to put them all out in the garden, which we usually do at feeding time, except when it's raining.

I looked towards the hall and there was a tri-coloured dog (black/tan & white). I was just about to shout my husband, to tell him he'd left one dog in the house, when I saw that the dog was (I find this hard to describe), like a shadow or very light mist. I could not really believe my eyes and must have blinked a few times. I got the strong impression it was my Moss. As soon as I said 'Mossy Boots', (I have nicknames for all my dogs and cats), he became very clear and I could see him as clear as I see someone real or as we see people every day.

I was so excited I just ran towards him to grab him to hug him but he then just disappeared. Of course I was shocked and thought I was seeing things. When my husband came in, I told him but he didn't believe me and I thought maybe it was wishful thinking on my part. I kept thinking, 'Moss has been dead for 15 years, why would I see him now if it was just wishful thinking?', as I was not thinking of him at the time.

The second of my dogs that I saw was one day when I was coming out of the bathroom. My other dogs were all in the hall wagging their tails, yet looking away from me. I took no notice and walked into the kitchen. The dogs all followed me as usual. Then for some reason, I went back into the hall and there was Rusty. He was not in a mist but as clear as day. I realised it was Rusty and not one of the other

Shelties I had lost because he was one of the most glamorous dogs I have ever owned and once seen, there was no forgetting him. I called out 'Russie Win' and went to pat him (will I ever learn?). The other dogs were all in the hall by then and went to greet him but he disappeared.

Again, as with Moss, I was so glad to see him but mad with myself for being so quick to rush at him.

The next dog I saw was my Sparky. He was also a tri-colour. I took his death very hard indeed. With my other dogs and cats that have gone, I have been lucky. They have not suffered long illnesses and in the end have gone quite quickly, even though we have had to have them all put to sleep, always taking our vet's advice when the final decision had to be made. We always stay with them, so that the last touch they feel is ours and the last voices they hear are ours.

Sparky had had several strokes in a week. On the Thursday he had another, which left him unable to stand. Our usual vet was not on duty that day and we saw a vet that we hadn't seen before. She said that Sparky was blind and paralysed down his left side. She wanted to increase his tablets but said that she did not think he would live much longer and would probably have more strokes. After a long discussion, my husband and I decided that it was not fair to let him go on. This was the first time that we had had to make that decision without help from our usual vet and we were extremely distressed.

That was in March. In July, a friend who had had one of my dogs, rang to tell me she had lost her Shelly. I was of course upset and was sitting thinking of Shelly and my other dogs and started to think about Sparky's death. I started to cry bitterly and was calling out Sparky's name. I felt a nudge on my leg.

Thinking it was one of my other dogs or cats, I cruelly said ' Go away, I want to be left alone', but the nudging carried on and when I looked down it was Sparky, so very clearly. I shouted 'Sparky Plug' and went to touch him but I could not feel him. He started to walk away but I called him not to leave me. I then got the distinct impression that he was not suffering and was happy in the spirit world with my mum and dad and other relatives and with our other dogs and cats. That was four years ago and I have not seen any of my departed animals since.

Of course, no one would believe me but I did feel better after seeing Sparky and my other dogs.

It is interesting to note that Moss is the father of Rusty and grandfather of Sparky.

Vicky

Gwen e-mailed me to say:

In 1990 I lost a most beloved Labrador, called Vicky. She was my first and we had a great bond. She was with me through some very bad times in my life and in fact saved my life.

When I lost her I was bereaved, there is no other word for it. I still fill up with my thoughts of her. I have had a few Labs since and loved them all so much but none like her.

When she died I couldn't get over it and some strange things happened. Vicky was the only dog to come into our bedroom but with her gone, I let her daughter Bea come in. She would never sleep on Vicky's side of the bed, as though she was still there and if she inadvertently went to lie there, it was as if she was booted out of the space.

One day I was going past the Spiritualist Church. I'd never been in one before but I decided to go to a service. I didn't get a message but it was a lovely happy place. Some weeks later, I had a private sitting with a visiting medium and took a tape to record my sitting. He was very accurate with much of what he said, including that my father had died young. Nearing the end of the session he said to me, quite clearly, 'Your dad has the Labrador.' Well, I just burst into tears. He went on to say that I had been on my knees asking my dad to look after her, which was exactly right. I had been on the floor with her and asked my dad to care for her for me.

When I came from there I could have flown home on cloud nine. I knew my beloved girl was safe with my dad.

*   *   *

Through Vicky, Gwen founded her own Labrador Rescue and has been involved in rehoming nearly 2000 Labradors. She wrote a beautiful poem which I include here, with her permission:

* * *

Do you think your heart is big enough, to store the love he gives,
this lovely pup you've just acquired, in the short time that he lives?
Do you think your heart is wide enough, to store up all the pride
of this handsome dog, all grown up, as he walks out by your side?
And will your heart be strong enough, to cope with all the pain,
when the time has come to say goodbye and you can't see him again?
Well when my heart's no longer strong and my life comes to an end,
there will be a celebration, 'cause I'll see my friend again.
As I take my walk down Heavenly shores, I know that I will see,
that familiar face, that wagging tail, waiting there for me.

* * *

In a second e-mail, Gwen had the following to say:

* * *

Some years ago, my best friend Karen had a little granddaughter, Emily, who was terminally ill. She also had an Airedale Terrier called Jess who was nearing the end of her life and Karen was distraught. Anyway, for some reason, Jess got a new lease of life from somewhere and saw my friend through the terrible trauma of losing her granddaughter who was only two. Jess managed a few months after Emily died and we all said that an angel gave her the extra time to see Karen through. I told my friend Mary and she wrote 'Jess's Gift' for her.

With Mary's permission, 'Jess's Gift' is included here:

* * *

The time had come for me to leave, quietly, I'd depart,
then I looked inside of you, saw pain etched in your heart.
I saw that you were grieving, sensed your trying times ahead,
so I asked if I could stay awhile, 'Of course you can', they said.

They gave me a new lease of life, they gave me added strength,
so the care and love you gave to me I could return at length.
I stayed there right beside you, you never were alone,
though my Angel waited patiently, to welcome me back home.

We got there together, we made it, you and I,
I hope I was your silver lining in your darkened sky.
And it really was so special, this extra time we had,
now look forward to the future; please mum, don't be sad.

So mum, I had to leave you, I could stay no more,
I had the fields and footpaths in Heaven to explore
but when you needed someone, someone to see you through,
my Angel said that I could give this special gift to you.

Mickey

Anne telephoned.

Anne has Clumber Spaniels amongst other dogs. She also takes in elderly cats and presently has 37. They are usually unwanted; strays, or from people who have died. Many of them have health problems through neglect or just simply old age. The biggest and most usual problem is kidney failure. All the cats are free to roam about the house as they please; never caged or confined in any way, as Anne likes them to have as natural a life as possible and all end their days with her.

One of these cats, named Mickey, had a very curly tail, 'like a Spitz dog', according to Anne. He was put to sleep at nine years of age, due to kidney failure. Anne says that he was also diabetic and in the end his kidneys just gave out.

Sometime after he was put to sleep, Anne was in her bedroom one day, when she saw a cat walk from the wardrobe, in a perfectly straight line, to disappear into a drawer in the chest of drawers. It was only later that she realized it was Mickey, because of its distinctive curly tail. She says that nothing like that had ever happened to her before.

*   *   *

Anne's friend Kim had two French Bulldogs. One was a thirteen-year-old male named Oliver; the other was a rescue named Jessie, who was thought to be around three years old. Two years ago, sadly, Jessie had kidney failure and had to be put to sleep. Soon afterwards, Kim saw her sitting underneath the settee and so, apparently, did Oliver, who reacted to her exactly as he would have done if she were still there in real life.

*   *   *

Other friends of Anne's quite clearly saw their cat Kesh, sitting by the Aga in the kitchen after he had been put to sleep.

Lovely Leah

Leah was an Irish Wolfhound. She was born on Christmas Day 1992, the smallest of a litter of twelve but always a fighter. Incredibly she outlived all her littermates and having attained her tenth birthday, died in February 2003. I know all this because I bred her. She was from my first litter of Wolfhounds and her new owners, Jane and Barry and I became good friends. At that time I was living in Norfolk. Sadly, over the years, we lost touch but when I moved to Wales six years ago, Barry tracked me down and now we do at least exchange Christmas cards!

Just after New Year 2004, Barry rang for a chat. In the course of the conversation he asked if I was still writing and I told him I was working on this book. He asked what it was about and when I explained he said "How strange, I had exactly that happen last Thursday when I was driving home".

He went on to say that he was driving along, quite normally, when he was suddenly aware that Leah was in the car with him. He said he wasn't thinking about her at the time or anything connected with her, in fact he wasn't thinking about anything in particular, just driving in a very relaxed manner, when he just knew that she was there with him. He said it felt completely natural and so real that he instinctively spoke to her as he would have done in this life; greeting her and asking how she was. He wasn't at all alarmed by it, being happy to have her there with him again, if only briefly.

Thinking about it afterwards, he did think it was strange that she got in the car with him, as in this life she rarely went anywhere in the car (except to the Vet's) and didn't really like it. (I'm not surprised Barry!)

A 'Phantom' Horse

Lucy had a dearly loved grey (white) mare called 'Phantom', who died at Christmas time in 2002 aged 37 years; a remarkable age for a horse, let alone one who had such a shaky start as this one!

Lucy was a teenager when she bought the mare in 1976 with savings of £150. Phantom was ten years old and according to Lucy, 'pretty skewed up in many ways, difficult to catch and shoe and very head-shy.' Out riding one day, Lucy was stopped by a gypsy, who recognised the mare because of her very distinctive striped hooves. He said she had belonged to a circus and because she wouldn't lunge, they had tied her to the back of one of the circus wagons and towed her along behind!

*   *   *

Lucy takes up the story:

I loved her with a passion. I cared for her daily for 27 years. She was never in a livery yard, so she looked to me for everything. I wouldn't like to guess how many rides we covered together. I can honestly say they were the happiest days of my life, out riding with my Phantom and Rhodie, my German Shorthaired Pointer.

At last the day I'd always dreaded arrived. Phantom collapsed in the field one day and was very dazed and confused. The vet said she had to be put to sleep. She was 37 years old and still I hadn't seen it coming. That was the 22nd. December 2002.

My husband arranged for her to be cremated but her ashes didn't come back for such a long time. We thought they had forgotten her, until, at the end of January 2003, we had a phone call from the gardener at the place where I used to keep her. He said 'Phantom's back, I've put her behind a tree.'

We went to the field and found her box and I carried it into her stable and said 'Come on girl.' I have to say I felt so fragile and broken hearted but somehow, when she returned in her lovely box, I felt much more at peace as if she was back in my care.

I was going to bury her but a friend said 'You can't bury a horse, they need to be free', so then began the long period of finding the right place to set her free and the right time.

My sister Sarah helped me find the right time. She lived in Canada but wanted to be there to say farewell to Phanty, so she asked me to wait until she was over for a visit, which was just before Easter. We kept putting off the evening; it had to be evening as my husband and daughter wanted to be there too; until the very last evening Sarah had before her return. It was Monday 7th. April and it was a stunning Spring evening, the best for weeks.

I had chosen the gallops above her field as the place to set her free. We picked an armful of daffodils from the driveway of the stables and when we got up to the gallops we found the absolute right place; a May bush in full bloom, the only white thing there.

We made it a jolly affair; planted a couple of trees and took handfuls of Phanty's ashes, throwing them high into the sky. The breeze carried the ash towards the May bush. It was really quite moving. Louis, my young G.S.P, jumped up to catch mouthfuls of this 'magic' ash. We took four photos with my sister's camera. My sister took the first three and I took the last one, (which was the last one on the reel of film), of my sister throwing the last of the ash high into the air.

As we turned to leave, we looked back at the May tree and watched the red sun disappear behind it. I can honestly say it was a very healing experience; so very right.

*   *   *

When her sister Sarah sent the developed photos from Canada, Lucy had quite a surprise. The first three all showed nothing more than dusty ash against the landscape but of the last one Sarah wrote in her letter 'Is Phantom taking one last look back at us?' This was the one Lucy had taken and it certainly looks like a grey horse galloping away from them, with its head turned back toward them, looking over its shoulder as if to say 'Goodbye'.

*   *   *

Lucy says:

'I don't feel her presence; I don't look for her or expect to see or feel her. I know she has moved on, galloped off to wherever it is our best companions go.'

Katy & Bo

Ruth has Pomeranian dogs. She e-mailed to say:

In the early nineties we lost a bitch called Katy. While she was alive we used to say she was too clever for her own good! Anyway, since she died we have often heard her barking upstairs and know for sure that no dog is there. When that does happen, when we go to bed we can see the impression of her on the bed in exactly the spot she lay on while alive. Not very long ago, my husband stopped in his tracks when going upstairs. He saw her coming down towards him as clear as could be and spoke her name and he said she looked up at him then vanished.

In 1997 we lost a dog we were all devoted to, called Bo. Nothing much happened but within a year his daughter died, aged only six and a half years. Basically she missed her dad and was broken hearted and never got over his loss. Within days of her death, I was working in the kitchen when something made me look up and there they both were coming out of our sitting room door, side by side as they always had and coming running towards me and out the kitchen door past me. I was struck dumb by it. This has happened several times since then. We often see them around the house and in the garden. Even visitors have asked who the two orange Poms are in the garden!

I have three daughters and three grandchildren and we have all seen what I have described. We all take comfort from it as I think we all feel that they knew how much they were loved and must have loved us just as much to keep calling on us. I feel I still have my three dogs around me. I don't think they will leave now. They were all dearly loved and were part of my family.

Last May (2002), I was given a great great grandson of Bo. When he came he barked like a normal Pom barks. Bo had a bark that was different from any other I have heard. Leroy, the new dog, now has exactly the same bark and I am continually saying, 'Be quiet Bo!' It is strange as he even answers to it as well.

Jewel & Tarot

Heather is a friend of mine who also has Wolfhounds. Earlier this year she lost two of her hounds, Jewel and Tarot, within a month. We only usually meet up at shows, so I hadn't seen her for a while and although I knew she'd lost Jewel, I had no idea that she'd lost Tarot as well. After I first sent a letter to Our Dogs, asking for contributions to this book, I received the following e-mail from her. This was just one more reason that I was convinced I had no choice in this; I had to write this book.

Heather's e-mail.

Hi – I've just read about your lads 'visits'. I lost both Jewel and Tarot last month. I am finding it really hard to cope about Tarot as she was dying – the vets never told me that. The way she was dying was awful. The liver was enlarged; all the fluid was seeping out of the blood vessels into the tissue. On the last day she could not drink and her tongue was drying up inside her mouth. I wish I had the peace to know that both she and Jewel are happy now.

*   *   *

I hope you do now Heather.

Ben

Vera sent an e-mail:

I know what I have to say isn't going to help much and is probably not what you want to hear but these are my thoughts on this extremely emotional subject.

Over the years since 1972, when we bought our first Basset, we have sadly had to say goodbye to a dozen of our dear friends. Furthermore, absolutely none has left us without our help at the end, which in some ways has made our partings even harder to live with. I am convinced that in every case we got it right; chose the right moment to make the dreadful decision to end their suffering while they still had a degree of dignity left. There has never been any occasion when I saw them afterwards.

There just might have been one occasion when something happened that some might consider an indication of a remaining presence. After Ben left us, the step outside the back door made the noise it makes when our hounds pass over it but nobody was out there. This happened just once.

I am not convinced about lurking spirits; an unbeliever if you like but devastating as each and every loss has been over the years (and apart from one hound, they have all lived well into their teens), I prefer to remain convinced that wherever they have gone, they are content and don't feel the need to return to be with us. This actually gives me far more peace than if I thought any of mine was so unsettled or perhaps unhappy that they felt they had to try to remain with us here.

*　*　*

Vera,
My personal opinion, based on our own experience and judging from the greater majority of the ADC accounts received, is that the reason our departed animals visit is more to do with our needs than theirs, coming to comfort those that are left behind, rather than because they are too unsettled or unhappy to move on. On the contrary, they seem to have a marvellous time in their new existence!

Mrs. T

Mrs. T telephoned.

Mrs. T and her family had an old-fashioned television set in a cabinet. Their cat used to climb up and sit on the corner of it, watched eagerly by the dogs who wouldn't dare touch her!

After the cat died, any ornaments placed on top of the cabinet would be pushed off onto the floor and the shields won by the dogs would be pushed away from the place where the cat used to sit.

The dogs would stare at the TV and then follow with their eyes as though the cat had jumped down from the cabinet and walked through into the next room.

Since the T family invested in a new television there have been no more incidents.

Spirit Dane

Debra e-mailed two photographs to me which she had taken using a Sony Mavica Digital Still Camera MVC-FD75.

The first, taken after dark on 24th August 2003, at her house, shows her mother's Great Dane dog, Hunter, who died in January 2003 from bloat. The second, taken earlier the same day, shows her own dog, Fidget, in the doorway. Debra describes Fidget as a cross-breed Heinz 57. She had been diabetic for two years prior to being put to sleep in June 2003. Both photos also show what appear to be human faces.

I asked Debra why she had taken photos of seemingly nothing more than her kitchen doorway and albeit one of those in the dark. She said she has lots of paranormal activity at her house and on this occasion she had heard her garage door slam shut for no apparent reason. At the same time, her linen basket was knocked over in the kitchen and a baking tray just flew off the kitchen work unit. She took the photos in the hope that she might catch something, which she obviously did. She is presently researching a murder that took place near where she lives and the negative spirit that is in her home is connected with the murder. As well as photographs, Debra also has video footage of the activity that occurs in her home.

Catching the dogs on film was a bonus. (Perhaps they feel that they still need to protect her house and family but from the other side now?)

Debra says she feels reassured that both her mum's dog and her own are safe and well and 'doing just fine' in the spirit world.

Rosemary Altea

Rosemary is a spiritual medium and healer. She is also the worldwide best-selling author of, The Eagle and the Rose *and* Proud Spirit.

*   *   *

Whilst doing some research one day, I took a book from my bookshelves, completely at random. This happened to be Rosemary's *Proud Spirit*. I had read it when I first bought it some years ago but hadn't looked at it since. I opened it somewhere in the middle and after reading two pages, was somewhat surprised to see my own Christian name staring at me as the heading for the next chapter, which made me think that perhaps I hadn't picked up this book 'just by chance'.

I went back to the beginning and started to read, thinking all the time that I must stop and go back to what I was intending to do originally. After ten minutes or so I came to a chapter titled 'Karma', the first three words of which were the question 'Do animals survive? I thought 'What!? I don't believe it.' and reading on, found that it was a wonderful ADC account of Rosemary's dogs, Karma and Jasper! Of course I must have read it before but so long ago that I had completely forgotten it and at the time, although it is fascinating reading, it would have had no relevance for me.

I lost no time in writing to Rosemary's Publishers, to ask if I could include the account in this book. With their permission it is reproduced here.

*   *   *

Karma

Karma died on June 1, 1994. As I buried him in the ground, under a huge rhododendron with enormous white blossoms, memories of our first meeting came to me. It was fourteen years ago, and my daughter, Samantha, then twelve and a half years old, had begged and pleaded for a dog, a King Charles Cavalier, a black-and-tan. She had been very specific about the breed and colour, but although I had scoured the country, I could not find a kennel that had what we wanted. Furthermore, each time I had asked Grey Eagle* for help, he showed me a picture of a puppy with long pale beige ears.

Well, I'm sure you know what's coming next. When all seemed lost and no puppies were to be found, I called the last kennel on the list. No, they couldn't help, but wait a moment – they knew of a woman who occasionally had litters. She didn't have a kennel, she bred from home. They gave me her name – Rix, Mrs Rix – but they didn't have her phone number. When I heard the name I connected it immediately with a client of mine. Could it be the same one? A long shot, but worth a try.

I looked it up in my files, found the phone number, and dialled. I spoke to a young girl who said she was Marie Rix's daughter and I tentatively asked if they were the Rixes who bred King Charles Cavaliers. "Yes" she said. "We've got a litter now, three bitches and one dog." I said I'd call later, and could she tell her mum that I was very interested in the dog. "Oh, yes," I breathed and asked the question I already knew the answer to: "What colour are they?" "Blenheim," replied the girl. "White and beige."

Marie Rix brought the pup to see us later that day. He was just two weeks old, so tiny he fitted into the palm of my hand. He was lively and wriggling, but when I placed him instinctively in the crook of my neck, he curled up and fell fast asleep.

Marie smiled. "We think we choose the dog," she said "but in reality it is they who choose, and I think Rosemary, that he just chose you."

---

* Grey Eagle is Rosemary's spirit guide.

Samantha was delighted and couldn't wait for the day we could bring him home. Four weeks later, Marie Rix called to tell us we could fetch him, two weeks earlier than we had originally planned. "He's driving his sisters crazy, chasing their tails and generally making a nuisance of himself," she laughed. "And quite frankly, you might find him a bit of a handful."

But I was not worried. After all, Grey Eagle had guided me to this pup – I felt sure of that. And so, nuisance or not, it was meant to be.

I named him Karma, from the Hindu word which means the force generated by a person's actions, or, as some might say, the life's breath. Force, energy, vibration, breath – whatever it is called, I felt that that force, that energy, was in part this small puppy, meant for me.

When he was not quite one year old I decided that he needed a companion, a playmate, and so I looked around and, with much less difficulty this time, found Jasper, another King Charles Cavalier. They instantly became friends, and I watched for the next three years as they grew and played together.

Although they were the same breed, it was amazing to me how different in character they were. Jasper was the lively, bouncy one, always ready to bound up onto my lap the moment I sat down, Karma, after his lively puppy days, was more sombre, a gentle and calm little dog.

When Jasper was two and a half and Karma a year older, I knew one of my boys was going to die. I was talking about them one day to a friend when I saw a vision, or rather more accurately, a picture, the spirit of Jasper, making its way heavenward. I was, of course, upset by the image. I asked Grey Eagle for more information, thinking that Jasper's death might be prevented if I could just know the circumstances, but I received no more details. I knew that what I had seen was one of life's inevitables.

However, hope lives eternal. Three months later, having caught and shaken to death a huge rat he had found in my orchard garden, Jasper had a major haemorrhage and almost died. (We discovered later that the rat had eaten some kind of poison.) I convinced myself this must be it, this must have been what I'd seen.

Two months later, when we had had bad storms and high winds, part of the fencing in the garden became dislodged, leaving a gap at the bottom, small enough to go unnoticed by me, but just big enough for an inquisitive little animal like Jasper to squeeze through. He ran out onto the road and straight in front of a truck.

The truck driver slammed on his brakes too late to avoid him, and Jasper lived just long enough to be placed into my arms, to hear my voice, soft and gentle, telling him I loved him. He looked at me one last time, then I saw his eyes glaze over. He took a deep breath, sighed, and was gone. My heart broken, I cried for days, and for many weeks, even months, every time we came into the house, Karma would race around, upstairs and downstairs, searching for his friend.

I had searched too, but in a different way, looking to see if I could catch a glimpse of Jasper in the spirit world. It was several months before I did so, and then it was quite unexpected. It was morning. Karma was sitting on the bed with me and I was about to get up when I felt something cold and wet on the back of my neck. Startled, I turned to see what it was, and saw Jasper, quite clearly. He put his nose into my hair, sniffing and pushing as he used to do. I felt his breath, and smelled him, and I saw Karma's reaction too. His tail was wagging nineteen to the dozen, and he was crying with excitement. For maybe ten minutes we were three together again, my boys and I. Then, just as quickly as he had come, my Jasper went again.

Often since that time over the years I glimpsed him and knew that he was safe and happy. I never got another dog, although I thought about it from time to time, but I felt that Karma was content, and so for the next ten years he was my only faithful companion.

As Karma grew older, his joints became stiff, he developed a heart murmur, and he became a bit of a creaking gate with a few aches and pains. But he was always, even in pain, a loving soul, a gentle-natured little boy.

Many times through the years I gave him healing. Not surprisingly, he was a very psychic little animal and would often, for no apparent reason, suddenly sit up and stare hard, either at the ceiling or in the corners of the room, his head moving sharply from place to place as if he were following some movement. People who didn't know us would find this quite unnerving, but I would smile and reassure them that it was only a visitor for Karma.

The last few months of his life he became more and more sick. His lungs had filled with fluid and his heart was weak. Each day, and several times a day, I gave him healing, which always calmed and comforted him. As always I would feel the centres of my palms grow warm and begin to throb, a sign that my energy was flowing, flowing from me to my little boy.

Karma was not a particularly pretty animal. He was cross-eyed, he smelled dreadful as he got older, and his hair came out in patches. But he was a gentle and loving little dog, and very special to me and to Samantha. When he became sick it was a comfort to me that in some small way, by placing my hands on him and using my energy, combined with God's energy, which I prayed for, I was able to ease his pain.

As you read this, I know that many of you who are animal lovers and have had sick pets, are wishing that in some way you too had the ability to give healing. And not just those of you who have animals, but those who have a loved one sick and in pain.

It is my belief that we all, to some degree, have the gift to heal, that we are born with that gift. When a child falls and grazes its knee, instinctively we gather up the child and, placing our hands on the injured spot, say, "Let me rub it better." If we have a headache, again, instinctively, our hands go to our brow and we may gently massage our temples. We have an innate ability, born to us, to give – by touch, by energy – healing. In my next book, titled *You Own the Power*, I will talk more of this and show how, by using simple exercises, we can develop this gift to some degree.

Eventually there came the day, that day which all of us who love our animals dread. It was time to make the final decision, one which I had prayed I would not have to make. It was not a surprise to me that Karma was dying, for Grey Eagle had warned me in advance, as he had with Jasper, and even given me the month. Again it was as in a vision that I saw my boy, lying, as if sleeping, outside on the grass, the sun bright, the month June.

I had seen this vision just less than one year before. Now here it was the beginning of June, and Karma had taken a distinct turn for the worse. I knew it had to be today. He couldn't lie down, he could hardly sit, and only managed to do so by propping himself against a wall. And when I looked at him I saw it in his eyes, his pleading: "Do something, help me."

As I dialled the number my heart felt leaden. How was I going to do this? I asked myself. Those of you who have been in a similar situation will know: you find the strength in love.

I took him out with me into the garden and laid him on my knee, my arms around him as I sat on the grass. When the vet brought the needle close to him I had one crazy moment when I wanted to shout out, "No, no!" But I bit my lip, and as tears coursed their way down my cheeks, I held my Karma more tightly to me, whispering lovingly to him. I watched as he died in my arms.

I didn't hear the vet leave – a friend had come, and had shown her out. I sat in quiet solitude for quite some time, not yet wanting to let go of this little animal who had been my friend for thirteen years.

Finally I laid him down, knowing that I must now take him to his most favourite place, the woods he loved to roam in, and bury him under the big white-blossomed rhododendron. As I returned to carry him to the car, I stopped and looked at him as he lay, seemingly peacefully asleep on the grass, and the vision Grey Eagle had given the year before came fully back to me, and I was comforted by the fact that it had been his time.

The house was now so empty. Samantha had left home two years earlier, and now my dog was gone. Each night I went to bed with my heart aching, for as smelly and mangy as he had been in his latter years, Karma always slept next to my bed, and my last act at bedtime, was to stroke him and say goodnight.

On the third night, in the middle of the night, I woke, turned over, and, as always, reached my hand down to the side of the bed to give Karma a reassuring pat. As I stroked him I murmured the usual love phrases: "It's all right, little boy, I'm here," and "Try and sleep now, I'll give you healing," and "Yes, yes, you're my beautiful boy."

It was only after several minutes that, realizing Karma was gone, I fully woke. With a start I sat up in bed, my hand, the hand I had been stroking Karma with, frozen in midair. And there I saw him, sitting upright by the side of the bed, half leaning against it as he always did. I reached out my hand to him and felt him under me, firm and solid, the hair on his head soft as silk through my fingers. He half turned his head and gazed at me, a contented look on his face. His breathing was strong and even, his breath warm and sweet.

One more time I stroked him, telling him as I did so that I loved my little boy. Then, a smile on my face, knowing my Karma had arrived safely and was happy, I lay down again and went to sleep.

The question? Do animals survive after death?

Well, as you can see from reading my story, yes . . . I believe they do.

Epilogue

It has certainly been a strange and in many ways, wonderful year; literally 'full of wonder'. Although this episode of our lives began in such tragic circumstances, it has led to a wealth of shared knowledge and experience. My fervent hope is that this book will give as much pleasure and comfort to those reading it, as it has given me in compiling it.

Many things have happened which I wouldn't have given a second thought to previously. All the rainbows (which I mentioned earlier) and strange butterfly activity for instance.

Before the first butterflies were about this year but a little while after we lost Sweep, I was walking back up the field with the dogs one evening, when a large white moth flew in front of my face and landed on the grass ahead of me. As we kept walking it flitted along the ground in front of us, completely unperturbed by the dogs. At the time, although I was unaware of butterflies and moths being spirit signs, it did make me wonder, because I thought it was such strange behaviour for a moth, so much so that I remembered it immediately when I later discovered its significance.

Once the butterflies would normally have been about, things were even stranger. We have a large garden with many flowering shrubs, including several varieties of Buddleia. Usually, each summer, the garden is full of butterflies of different kinds. This year, at any one time, there has only ever been a single Red Admiral, sometimes accompanied by a single white butterfly. Indoors, many times when I have been upstairs in our bedroom, a single Red Admiral has appeared, seemingly from nowhere, and fluttered against the Velux window, almost as if to attract my attention. Several times I have opened the Velux to let it out and it has flown in again through the open window on the opposite side of the bedroom. Downstairs, there has often been a single Red Admiral accompanying me in the office, or the barn, whenever I have been working on this book.

I know it hasn't always been the same Red Admiral, because on one occasion, in the kitchen this time, I caught it to put it outside and noticed that both of its wings were damaged. On other occasions the wings have both been perfect but the butterfly with the damaged wings has also been upstairs on the Velux.

When we went to Ireland in August, we had a Red Admiral accompanying us in the van and when we stopped at a pub for lunch, we sat at a table just inside one of the windows and after a few minutes what should appear fluttering against the outside of the window but a Red Admiral.

In November, when we thought all the butterflies had gone into hibernation, we were sitting in the lounge one night when suddenly, there was a Red Admiral zooming round the room like a mad thing! We didn't see it come in, goodness only knows where it came from and we didn't see it leave, it just flew down towards the floor and it was gone.

Now of course, all this butterfly activity could be perfectly normal behaviour for butterflies. I have to confess I've never studied them before and don't know what's normal and what isn't as far as they're concerned but it seems strange to me that all the activity has been confined to just one at a time (except when the white one has been present). Anyway, it's kept us amused and we always say 'Hello again, how are you?' whenever we see one.

Despite there being just one live butterfly about at a time until November; from December onwards suddenly there appeared, again seemingly from nowhere as we didn't see them arrive, no less than four dead Red Admirals (at once) on the lounge windowsill, four more on the bedroom windowsill and two behind the headboard of our bed!

The next strange thing was when we came back from Ireland in June. When we arrived home, the first thing our dogsitter said when she opened the gate was 'What time did your ferry get in?' 'About one o'clock' I said, 'Why?' 'Thought so' she said, 'The dogs all started howling then and I couldn't think of any other reason'. How did they know? The ferry is a good hour and a half's drive from home. They've never done it before when we've been away.

Then there's the mighty strange effect I seem to have been having on all things electrical. It began with the starter motor in the old VW runabout van we had. Every time I went to start it, it would just go 'click' and that would be it. Steve would get in, turn the key and away it would go. Then it was the Granada car. We went to Wolverhampton to fetch a lorry. Steve drove there but as he obviously had to drive the lorry back, I had to drive the car. We'd been stopped for quite some time while he checked the lorry over. When we were ready to head for home he told me to turn the car round and follow him. I switched it on, 'click', nothing! The starter was jammed.

Next was the lorry. Steve was adjusting the brakes one day and asked me to sit in it and press the brake pedal. He told me to start it up to build the air up. I switched it on, 'click'. I can't repeat what Steve said!

Then, out shopping one day, we were in Littlewoods store and I took my goods to the counter to pay. I gave the girl behind the counter my credit card and she ran it through the machine but when she went to open the electric till – it was jammed. It took twenty minutes to sort that one out.

At home, the computer is always shut down last thing at night. It shuts down first time every time for Steve. Nine times out of ten it refuses to shut down for me, no matter how carefully I go through the procedure.

At the moment, things seem to have settled down a little, (touch wood). Perhaps now I'm nearing the end of this book I'm not quite as electrically charged as I was!

*   *   *

Oh dear, spoke too soon! While I was reading this through, prior to going to print, the phone rang. It was Steve to say he was on his way home in the lorry. He was just chatting away (on the hands-free of course) and eventually, because I wanted to get on, I said 'Tell me all this when you get home, I'm trying to get on with the book.'

'OK,' he said.

Five minutes later he rang again. 'What do you want now?' I said.

'I've broken down,' he said.

'You're joking. You are joking aren't you?'

'No I'm not. It just boiled but the engine isn't hot.'

'Don't like the sound of that. What do you think it is?'

'Don't know but I'll wait a few minutes to see if it cools down and try to limp home.'

I said 'That's quite strange really because I was just re-reading the bit I'd written about all the electrical things going wrong.'

(Can't repeat the next bit.)

It turned out to be the water pump, which, I'm informed, is actually mechanical rather than electrical but I still got the blame, needless to say!

For the Future

A lthough some of the accounts in this book are from respected Mediums, it must be obvious to all that you don't have to be a Medium in order to have an ADC experience. They can and do happen to anyone. It seems the only thing needed is love, on either side.

If you were sceptical or a non-believer before reading this book, I hope it has, at least, given you food for thought. But – if you think it is all just imagination, or wishful thinking, do you also think it's logical that so many people have all imagined the same thing? (Even if they've all wished for it?) I do *not* profess to be any kind of expert on the subject, just someone who has been deeply moved by our own experience, who wanted to share that with others and who now wants to find out more.

So, whether you are a believer or not, I would be pleased to hear your views and any thoughts you may have regarding the contents of this book.

I hope to do a further book of ADC accounts, so please continue to send your experiences to me. Some of the later ADC's contained in this book raise issues that I hope to explore in greater depth in a future book.

For instance, the subject of reincarnation. Do you have, or have you ever had, an animal which you believe to be the reincarnation of a former one? Have any of your animals, past or present, taken on characteristics belonging to a deceased animal, which they didn't have before that animal passed?

Interestingly enough, I was watching a recent John Edward programme, when right at the end someone asked him what he thought about reincarnation. One of the things he said was, (in a nutshell) that if a young child says things about someone that has passed, that they couldn't possibly have known; or adopts mannerisms that that person had; they are automatically assumed to be the reincarnation of that person.

John said that instead of that being the case, he feels it is more likely that the child is acting as a medium for the deceased person's spirit to make contact. When they say or do things that identify them with the deceased, it is merely that person's spirit trying to offer validation of their presence. Phew!

It is a recognised fact that young children are naturally psychic and so personally, I think it is quite feasible that they could act as Mediums. We are all born with that ability but because most of us don't use it, quite simply, as we get older we lose it. Is there any reason to suppose that animals are less psychic than young children? They have demonstrated time and time again (as with our own dogs when we returned from Ireland in June 2003) that they have a sixth sense. Is it possible then, that they could act as mediums for other, deceased animals?

Do you think that what John said makes perfect sense, or do you believe it is more likely that they are reincarnated? Please, let me have your thoughts on the subject, along with any accounts of animal/s that you believe are, or have been reincarnated, or, which have adopted traits belonging to a deceased animal.

*   *   *

Have you caught anything in a photograph that you didn't realise was there when you took it, or could explain afterwards? Please let me have copies (which will be returned) with as much detail as possible about the events surrounding each photo.

*   *   *

Have any of your animals ever displayed a real sixth-sense or telepathy? Again, please let me have your stories with as much detail as possible.

*   *   *

And finally

Have you had any unusual happenings in the way of butterflies, moths, feathers, rainbows, birds etc., or smells; anything that you feel might have been a sign from a departed animal?

You can write to me at:

Penlleinau, Blaencaron, Tregaron, Ceredigion, Wales SY25 6HL.

Or telephone me on:
(01974) 299000

Or E-Mail me at:
RYNCHANON@NIGHTWING.FSBUSINESS.CO.UK

Bibliography

ALTEA Rosemary – *Proud Spirit*. 1997. Published by Rider. The Random House Group Ltd.

ANGELO Jack – *Your Healing Power*. 1999. Published by Piatkus.

GUGGENHEIM Bill & GUGGENHEIM Judy – *Hello From Heaven*. 1995. Published by Bantam Books.

MOONDANCE Wolf – *Spirit Medicine*. 1995. Published by Sterling Publishing Company Inc.